EILEEN GERSHON is married  up children and five grandc her life. Every day she uses as a nurse, including a strict there is nothing that brings others and believes the more

She continues to work hard and play hard. She loves her home, the Scottish Highlands, beautiful clothes and champagne. She is a member of her local WI where she has been President many times. She has enjoyed years of tap dancing and she wishes she was better at playing the piano. Her favourite pastime is collecting friends.

To find out more, visit her website: www.eileengershon.com.

Nurses Never Run

EILEEN GERSHON

SilverWood

Published in 2015 by SilverWood Books

SilverWood Books Ltd
14 Small Street, Bristol, BS1 1DE, United Kingdom
www.silverwoodbooks.co.uk

Copyright © Eileen Gershon 2015
Images © Eileen Gershon 2015
Hospital images © Addenbrooke's Hospital Archives

The right of Eileen Gershon to be identified as the author of this work
has been asserted by her in accordance with the
Copyright, Designs and Patents Act 1988.

All rights reserved. No part of this publication may be reproduced,
stored in a retrieval system, or transmitted in any form or by any means,
electronic, mechanical, photocopying, recording or otherwise,
without prior permission of the copyright holder.

ISBN 978-1-78132-409-7 (paperback)
ISBN 978-1-78132-410-3 (ebook)

British Library Cataloguing in Publication Data
A CIP catalogue record for this book is available from
the British Library

Set in Adobe Garamond Pro by SilverWood Books
Printed by Latimer Trend on responsibly sourced paper

*Mother saved my letters and returned them to me
years later, saying, "You should write a book."
It is too late for her to read it, but her support still
feels constant and her love endless. This is for her.*

Acknowledgements

This book is autobiographical.

I must thank Peter for his encouragement and his willingness for me to include personal details of the early days of our life together. He makes it easy for me to love him 'always and forever'.

Without the letters saved by both Mother and Peter this book would have been a lot more difficult to write. I owe them a debt of gratitude. I have taken the liberty of condensing, amalgamating, and putting to one side many of the letters because I wrote most days and there is an overwhelming pile of them. I have added in some memories that escaped record at the time. The names of patients are deliberately omitted to ensure confidentiality and the names of all my boyfriends prior to Peter have been altered for anonymity.

I am grateful to all my family and friends who have helped by reading drafts for being both encouraging and constructive in their criticism.

Every writer needs an editor, but I needed someone to teach me how to write a book, to challenge me to rewrite, make improvements and strive for a higher standard. Fleur has fulfilled that role perfectly and been generous with both her time and her expertise. I hope she understands how much I appreciated her help and how glad I am to have made a new friend.

Then SilverWood took my manuscript and turned it into a real book. It is both an heirloom for my grandchildren to read in the future, and a fundraiser to benefit Acorn House and Chestnut House at Addenbrooke's Hospital. I wish to express my appreciation to Helen Hart (publishing director) and

Bronwen Wotton (publishing assistant) for being professional, helpful and friendly. Also my thanks go to the design team for an eye-catching cover, and to all the other people who have worked hard on my behalf.

Lastly, and most important of all, I must thank all my nursing colleagues, and their boyfriends, for allowing me to use their real names and tell part of what is their story too. Their friendship during that challenging three and a half years, and beyond, has been very special and full of kindness and laughter. I look forward to many more happy reunions.

NURSES NEVER RUN

Preliminary Training School

8th September 1967

I'm enjoying absolutely everything and I don't feel the slightest bit homesick, it's as if I've been here ages. Everyone is very friendly and different groups don't keep to themselves, in fact most of the first years chat with us and are very helpful answering questions, which is lucky as we've got lots to ask!

Everyone else seems to eat a lot quicker than me, probably because I talk the most.

It was exciting to get not one, but two wolf-whistles down the town; something to do with my long legs, a miniskirt and a bicycle, I guess!

Every day was full of excitement. My hand flew across the paper as words poured from my fountain pen. I wanted to share the experience and my brain needed to make sense of all that was happening. My new independence, albeit limited, was both thrilling and daunting. The world of illness and death would prove challenging, but life in Cambridge was full of opportunities, and boys! Letters were my lifeline, a pleasure to write, a joy to receive, and an efficient means of communication in an era when telephone calls were expensive and only used for matters of importance.

Here I was embarking on a career I had always wanted. I arrived at Owlstonecroft, the Nurses' Home and Preliminary Training School (PTS) for Addenbrooke's Hospital, on the afternoon of 4th September 1967 with forty-nine other equally apprehensive girls. We had all been through the interview process over a year ago. Mine was on 1st June 1966, and by 3rd June a letter had been despatched accepting me for training. I remember I was asked why I wanted to be a nurse. I replied that I didn't have a reason, I had simply always known that was what I wanted to do. That was presumably the right answer!

Owlstonecroft was a functional building with a car park and bike sheds in front and grass with tennis courts to the side. There were no flowerbeds to soften the austere image. As we climbed out of family cars and rescued our bikes and suitcases we sneaked sideways glances at each other, and I noted only one other girl was wearing a miniskirt like myself. I wondered if I would find like-minded friends amongst this conservatively dressed crowd. Had they, like me, made patients of their dolls and been fascinated by hospitals and doctors' surgeries? Had they experienced the magic of sitting up all night with their mother, doing jigsaws in the glow of the bedroom's gas fire, helping to care for their siblings who were delirious with the fever of measles? Did their sixth form teachers look down on them in a mystified way, wondering why they were studying for A levels if they planned to be a lowly nurse and had no intention of going to university? Was Addenbrooke's their first choice, or had they also applied to, and been rejected by, a famous London hospital, and did that matter? Surely we were all hoping Cambridge would be an inspiring, special, and beautiful place to live and knew the hospital had a renowned reputation for training excellent nurses. Had they considered the boys? They had to have noticed that ten lads to every girl offered odds full of promise! Did we all have a vocation? It was a mystery to me. What did it really mean and how did we know if we had it? Despite the numerous questions, we smiled bravely at each other, bade farewell to our families with false cheerfulness and entered our new home.

Visitors were discouraged beyond the front door, and men were *not allowed*. There was a bleak visitors' room next to Home Sister's office, but as she seemed always to be there and listening, it was invariably empty. She was (like most home sisters) unmarried, older, had retired from the wards and lived in the Nurses' Home. She guarded us like a dragon and was feared and avoided whenever possible.

We were shown to the modern extension. We each had our own room with basic furnishings, a narrow single bed with side table, a wardrobe, a desk and a wash-hand basin. The toilets, bathrooms, kitchenette and laundry were along the corridor. We were expected to keep our rooms tidy and to strip and change our beds fortnightly. The maids cleaned the rooms, and Home Sister made unannounced inspections. The tiny wardrobe was adequate as we possessed few clothes. I owned a pair of jeans, two skirts and blouses (one set of which I was wearing), a couple of jumpers and two brand new dresses I'd made for best. I had two pairs of shoes with slingbacks and fashionably low heels (not to mention the boring brown lace ups for work), and one coat. My underwear included the necessary but uncomfortable suspender belts and natural shaded stockings. Tights had just appeared in the shops, but were too expensive for everyday wear, though we soon worked out that you could cut off the laddered leg and wear two half pairs together to make them last longer. It didn't take long to unpack, put everything away and pile the recently purchased text books on the desk. The curtains were green and blue check and not unpleasing, but I was amused to notice the windows were secured so that they would only open a crack to let in fresh air. We were assured this was for our protection as we were on the ground floor and no one could climb in. Equally we were imprisoned and had to sign out and in again at the porter's desk by 11pm. Occasional late passes were granted until midnight, with a special extension for the Hospital Ball. If we were late we were grounded, and Home Sister stood at the door, looking at her watch as we threw our bikes into the racks and raced to beat the curfew.

But I'm ahead of myself…we have only just arrived and are tentatively introducing ourselves. Gill is in the room next door; we say hello and are soon chatting amicably. Within minutes we discover our parents live quite near each other in Essex and so we will be able to share lifts, or travel together on the trains, when we go home. I hear that Gill has an older sister and brother, and she learns I am the second of five children. We discover we have a lot in common as we have both been well educated in the state system and have had happy childhoods where there was sufficient money for basics, but not enough for many luxuries. Together we go to find the communal lounge where a cup of tea is served prior to a welcome speech from Home Sister. We meet Angie and she introduces us to Liz whose room is near hers.

We are all impressed by Dawn who becomes the centre of attention. She stands poised, full of confidence, and with her immaculate salon-set fair hair she appears more grown-up. She's been on a Pre-Student Nursing Course and has already mastered the basic skills and has even seen a dead body! She not only drives a car, but also has a steady boyfriend called Alan. Dawn is very friendly, but most of us are a little bit in awe of her.

To our surprise we discover we get all the weekends off whilst in PTS, and nearly everyone queues at the payphone to make plans to go home. We descend on the dining room for supper and meet some of the first years who live in the older part of the Nurses' Home and bombard them with questions.

Before long I'm continuing the letter to my parents and my younger two brothers and sister. I wrote separately to my big brother, Paul, as he no longer lives at home.

At the moment we are in PTS and working from 8.15am–4.15pm. We get half an hour for coffee and one hour for lunch. It is exhausting, much harder than High School, and we all feel like flopping on our beds and going to sleep afterwards. However, we've been instructed not to do this and to train ourselves to manage on only eight hours sleep, because otherwise once we get on the wards and work shifts we won't cope.

An A shift is 7.30am–4.30pm, a B shift is 1.30pm–9.30pm, and worst of all a split shift is 7.30am–1.30pm and 6.30pm–9.30pm all in one day!

The sister tutors claim if we get used to sleeping lots then we will soon find we have no time for anything except work and sleep, get into a rut and crack up physically and mentally. I've decided never to ask for a late pass unless I am off the next day, or not working until the afternoon, then I can have a lie-in.

I'll let you have the numbers of the two payphones outside the dining room. Anyone nearby could answer so it is easiest if you give them a message and they will put it in my pigeon hole. I'll soon spot it as I check for post every time I go by.

It felt strange being called Nurse Walker. PTS lasted eight weeks and took place in the adjacent school building where we had lectures, classroom sessions seated at desks and practical lessons in a mock three bedded ward. Practicals were fun as we took each other's temperature, pulse, respirations and blood pressure. We learnt to make beds correctly with hospital corners, tucking the sheets in and loosening the top sheet slightly to relieve pressure on the toes, with the pillow case openings facing away from the door and the bed wheels locked and facing inwards. We discovered the art of positioning the four or five pillows to make the patient comfortable, whether sitting supported by the back rest or lying on their side, and when to use a cradle to keep the weight of the blankets off the legs. We mastered the technique of lifting patients safely and transferring them to trolleys or chairs whilst leaving the top bedcovers in a neatly folded pack which could be removed and replaced with minimum fuss. We practised giving the perfect injection into oranges, both intra-muscular into the upper outer quadrant of the buttock and subcutaneous for insulin injections. We learnt how to measure and test urine, pass Ryles tubes for nasogastric feeding, and how to prevent and treat pressure sores.

"What are pressure sores, Nurse? Pressure sores are a sign of *bad nursing*!"

"Do it once, Nurse, and do it *properly*!"

"Nurses *never run*!"

"Don't put it down, put it *away*!"

"Why? Nurse, *why*?"

The sister tutor's words resound to this day as she stressed the importance of accurate charting and explained the mysteries of drugs and doses. We were taught all the basic tasks we would perform every day on every ward and were given enough confidence to be quick and efficient. We were uncomfortably aware that most patients cannot tell a raw recruit from an experienced nurse, despite the multitude of different uniforms, and we needed to be reassured that we were all capable and adequately prepared for life on the wards.

Letter home:

12th September 1967

Now I have a number painted on my bike's rear mudguard I feel I belong and am part of the Cambridge scene. Last night I went to see The Taming of the Shrew at the Arts Cinema, where nurses get free tickets if there are unsold seats. We can get these at the Arts Theatre too, ten pin bowling, reductions for punts and almost anything in Cambridge if we whisper "Nurse" in the right ear and smile. This is going to be brilliant as we could hardly afford to go otherwise. You know I love everything about the theatre and I'm planning to go as often as I can.

We get tested every Friday and are expected to get over 50 per cent or out! I still have not got the rest of my uniform and have had to wear this dress for two weeks. I hope the new one comes before we venture to the wards on Friday morning.

Only eight of us stayed here at the weekend and I showed some of them around, a chance to air my limited knowledge of Cambridge. We cycled along The Backs to Trinity and then went on to see the Round Church. The others were impressed I knew my way around.

My father had been at Trinity College and my mother was a Cambridge dairy farmer's daughter. I was born in my grandmother's house in Girton village and baptised at the Round Church. Although we moved to Essex when I was eighteen months old, we visited Cambridge on many occasions and I inherited my parents' love of the city.

Gill was one of the nurses who stayed that first weekend and we had more time to get to know each other. The beginning of a close friendship. We tried on each other's dresses and, although I was taller, we decided to share most of our clothes (though not shoes), extending our wardrobes considerably. Luckily we have the same colouring with long dark brown hair, hazel eyes, skin that tans easily and a slim build. We were so alike that on several occasions at parties, admittedly where alcohol was flowing freely, we were mistaken for sisters, and even identical twins! We chatted endlessly, exploring our similar outlook on life, sharing our feelings and putting the world to rights.

Our uniform was provided and laundered weekly free of charge. All student nurses at Addenbrooke's wore identical dresses, and within days we had shortened the hems to knee length. They were of heavy cotton, thinly striped in mauve and white, with concealed buttons up the front from hem to neck, detachable starched white collars, short sleeves and breast pockets for the essential red and blue biros, scissors on a chain that clipped to the waist, spare white kirby grips to hold our hats on and often safety pins too. Sooner or later all of us acquired a pair of Spencer-Wells artery forceps as a useful extra (invaluable when dealing with drips and catheters) to add to the collection in our pockets. Aprons fastened around our waists with detachable buttons and the bib was safety pinned by tabs to our dresses. Aprons were removed for all break periods and were never worn outside the hospital. We soon learnt to keep a spare clean one to hand for a quick change following a messy disaster, and that the underside of the apron's hem was invaluable for writing memos as it was easier to access than the notebook in the skirt pocket and the boil wash at the laundry erased them. As students we wore white paper card hats and our hair had to be off our shoulders and neat and tidy at all times. Our navy cardigans were for warmth whilst traversing hospital corridors during breaks and were never worn at the same time as an apron. This rule we broke blatantly during the quiet, chilly hours of night duty, whipping them off quickly if we heard Night Sister approaching. We wore navy gabardine raincoats over our uniforms outdoors, and most of us bought a hospital scarf as soon as we were entitled to, being successfully through PTS and officially accepted for training. Just like the university college scarves, they were warm and long enough to cover our heads, ears and necks, efficiently protecting us from the cold easterly winds. We were proud to wear the Cambridge blue with the white and purple stripes of the hospital, a status symbol and an essential part of our identity.

We rarely wore uniform to go into town, only to and from work as there were no proper changing facilities at the hospital. We were disappointed to discover cloaks and bicycles don't work, and certainly would not have been safe. Sadly we never had those glorious red lined capes with the criss-cross straps, although there were still a few around owned by the older ward sisters and shamelessly borrowed by us on night duty when we were third years and felt we could get away with it. But that level of confidence was unimaginable as I ventured onto a ward for the first time.

Letter home:

18th September 1967

On Friday we visited the wards in small groups with the Clinical Instructor. We went to Goode (gynaecology) and bed bathed a lady who had recently had a hysterectomy. She was only thirty-seven, which is young for that operation. I found her easy to talk to as I dried her arm and chest and even washed a leg. Later we helped to give out the lunches, which are served up on the ward from a heated trolley by the sister, and we helped to feed some of the patients. Afterwards we did the bedpan round; you wouldn't think that was very exciting, but we loved it all. It's amusing practising on each other in the school, but much more interesting with genuine patients.

The test was horrible. We didn't get any anatomy questions, which I'd thought was a dead cert, and instead we had to write out the bed bath procedure, which I thought was easy until I tried to put it down on paper. Anyway I don't think I've made any dreadful boobs.

At last I have got some more of my uniform which, blessings all round, fits much better. I just need to sew on all the name tapes and shorten the hems of the dresses, of course.

Last weekend I made a grand tour of the best known colleges to get to know Cambridge better. Both King's and Trinity's chapels have scaffolding and are being cleaned, and the town's filling up with undergraduates, hoorah! We are so busy we hardly ever go to the television room except for, you guessed it, Top of the Pops. We play table tennis and have coffee parties in each other's rooms. It's my turn next so I need to buy some coffee and biscuits; milk is provided in the kitchenette. Gill's coming, of course, and I've invited Angie and Liz so we can all get to know one another better. I did ask Dawn, but she has already agreed to go to a party in Annie's room. Quite naturally our set seems to be dividing into smaller groups in a very amicable way.

The first thing we noticed about Liz was her attractive laugh echoing down the corridor; her merriment was infectious. She was extrovert with a wicked sense of humour, probably just as well as she was one of twins with five other siblings. She had short dark hair and was of medium height and build. Within minutes I felt I had known her for ages and could sense a lot of fun would radiate from her in the days ahead. She and I slipped easily into the happy banter that is prevalent in big noisy families, little knowing that one day we would become members of the same family.

Angie was different. She was very quiet, almost silent. I found this unnerving at first as I had always surrounded myself with equally chatty people. This was a new experience: someone who obviously wanted to be part of the group, but did not join in spontaneously. Was she painfully shy? Angie was of a similar height to Liz, but had short blonde curly hair. She sat completely still, listening rather than volunteering an opinion. After a while we discovered she was happy to answer questions and contribute if invited to do so. This way we learnt that her parents had been killed in a tragic car accident, and now she and her little brother lived with their uncle and aunt. Her uncle was a vicar, as was Gill's father which gave them a common bond.

Later in the evening, as Angie relaxed we found she had a hilarious dry wit. Quick as a flash, Liz, Gill and I would pick up on it and giggle helplessly. Laughter dominated our future get-togethers and kept us in high spirits. We all shared the sense of humour that is typical of nurses (also doctors, the police, firemen and ambulance services): we had the ability to see the funny side of life even in its darkest hours.

27th September 1967

Dearest Darling Daddy,

Please, I can't fill in my ridiculous tax form without your valuable assistance. Could you pencil in the necessary figures and let me have it back to ink in and sign? I think what I've done is right, but I'm not sure. It strikes me that none of the form is applicable to me at all, and no one deems it necessary to explain tax, National Insurance or superannuation to us. How are we supposed to understand it all?

Thursday afternoon I have to venture to the New Site where I am to work on Ward 4 (orthopaedics). Apparently it has lots of small six bed units off a corridor with different bays for men, women and children. The new hospital doesn't have the long Nightingale wards. I feel a bit apprehensive as I told one of the first years I was starting there and she said, "Throwing you in the deep end, are they?" There are often seriously injured car crash victims, but not the head injuries, small mercy, as they go to a different ward. Apart from the extra travelling I consider myself lucky to be starting at the New Site because I'll have all the advantages of the newer equipment. I go there once, and then twice, a week until the end of PTS, and then I will do my first eight weeks training on that ward. I'm looking forward to it very much, but I must admit I am terrified too. I feel horribly inadequate.

Addenbrooke's Hospital New Site, stage 1, was opened by the Queen in May 1962. It housed Outpatients, Accident Service, X-ray, a four ward block of two neurological wards and two orthopaedic wards with the appropriate theatres above. All this was connected by underground walkways, with storage rooms and the necessary mortuary, to a small residency and dining rooms for the staff. From Owlstonecroft, which was in Newnham village, we cycled to the Old Site on Trumpington Street and caught the hospital transport, a minibus, to the New Site on Hills Road.

Letter to all at home:

2nd October 1967

Apologies for short letters, but honestly I'm so busy. I am now halfway through PTS and in the last test I got 19/25 and 21/25, but the results this week will be a different story because we got a bacteriology question and I hadn't even looked at that when I revised, oops!

My second afternoon on Ward 4 went fine. I did the men's bottle round all by myself and I watched a dressing being changed on a foot with gangrene. Well it is supposed to be a foot, but personally I have my doubts. There were only two toes left, the skin was all black with huge holes revealing bone, ugh! The patient is great fun and is a right flirt, which the nurses play along with to keep his spirits up. He is nursed in isolation, and I felt I looked the part in a gown and mask (which helped because the smell was horrible).

I've never washed my hands as often as we do now. We quip, "If in doubt, wash your hands!" I worry I'll get a man to bed bath tomorrow; hopefully he'll be more embarrassed than me.

Our first pay cheque was very disappointing. Our annual salary is £365 and we over-optimistically expected to get £1 a day and had rather forgotten they would take off our board and lodging, tax, Nat. Ins. and superannuation. We certainly hadn't bargained for them deducting the cost of our files and paper too and we were left with hardly anything at all.

Never mind, the good news is it looks as if I'll be able to get time off for the High School Prize Giving in December as Sister lets us have any days off that we request, as long as we don't ask too often and she can arrange it. I'm looking forward to coming home and seeing you all on Friday.

Stop press news: Gill and I have been elected set representatives for regular meetings with the powers that be, including Matron! I do seem to lay myself open to making myself unpopular with those in authority; thank goodness I've got Gill to back me up. They probably chose us because we are friends and not backward about coming forward!

Gill and I were two born leaders. We were confident, articulate, could think quickly and react promptly to changing circumstances. We were both practical and down to earth, Gill even more so than me! Already we could glance across a room and know what the other was thinking. We made a good team.

Letters home:

10th October 1967

Thank you for giving me a restful weekend, and thank you, Mummy, for your letter: I am glad your budgerigar died quietly and did not suffer. It is a strange coincidence that the day you buried him in the garden we were learning about Care of the Dying and Last Offices.

At the moment I am off duty until 1.15pm, and then I have to work until 9.30pm by which time I shall probably be dead on my feet. I am sitting under the dryer after a rather necessary hair wash. My hair seems to get much dirtier here, I suppose because I have to keep putting it up and taking it down again. Letting your hair down when you come off duty gives that expression a whole new relevance!

Things are looking up now the undergrads have arrived. Poor Prince Charles is having rather a tough time with hundreds of photographers everywhere. I haven't seen him, mainly because I haven't been putting myself out to find him; besides I feel sorry for him with all this fuss and commotion, poor lad. It was really funny cycling down from Owlstonecroft yesterday as there were two pairs of undergrads strategically placed and obviously wanting to look over the new intake of nurses. We waved to them.

The Hospital Shadow Ball is on Friday 20th October (double tickets £27) and I shall most definitely go, but small problem of a partner. Surely I can find someone?

15th October 1967

I have been doing so much and having such a fabulous, glorious, wonderful time that it is difficult to find time to write, and there is so much to say I hardly know where to start.

Cambridge is full of tempting undergrads and Gill and I are doing our best to meet all 10,000 of them. Gill started going out with her boyfriend, Henry, in Newcastle-under-Lyme when they were still at school, but they have agreed she is free to see other boys until he comes up next year. She's sure she won't meet anyone whom she likes better, but she is prepared to look! I still haven't seen Prince Charles, but when there are so many other boys there simply isn't time to go searching for one. There are literally hundreds of parties (coming up parties, freshman dances, staircase parties) and it is impossible to fit all the invitations in. I met my first undergrad on Monday and got asked out on Tuesday, not bad eh? He's called Robert and is tall, dark and handsome.

This week is going to be hectic but promises to be lots of fun. Tonight I'm writing letters, copying up notes from lectures, having a bath and early bed. Tomorrow we are shopping in the morning, but on duty in the afternoon. Wednesday I'm seeing

Robert and Thursday I'm going to watch some of a nursing colleague's friends who play in a band. Then it is Friday and the Shadow Ball. In the end I asked Patrick. I know I said I'd stop seeing him when I came to Cambridge, but he turned up one weekend armed with flowers and a huge box of chocolates, which the others helped me eat! He's agreed to come up for the night and hire a dinner jacket. I'm not sure it is really fair of me to encourage him when I'd rather meet new people, but he is reliable and I know we'll have a good time together. I've decided to treat myself to a gorgeous Edwardian style white blouse to go with the long black velvet skirt I've made, as that is absolutely the in thing. What a marvellous life we lead. I'm so glad I came to Cambridge.

I have done two complete shifts on the wards. Both were interesting but very tiring. An A is the more exhausting as you have to stay alive after you come off duty at teatime, whereas after a B you can just fall into bed. I've given bed baths by myself and managed a complete bedpan round single handed. I've seen a traction pin removed, pulled straight through a man's leg, ugh! I've been up to the theatre ante-room and to Assistant Matron's office. (This involves walking across a passageway suspended in mid air three floors up between two buildings in the rain and the wind. Not good for my vertigo, I had to look straight ahead and walk very quickly!) At last I've met the ward sister. She's about twenty-seven, young compared to most sisters, and works with her staff which is nice. She's a stickler for getting things done quickly and properly, which is doubtless a good thing.

It's salad for supper tonight. Angie's pleased; she worries about her shape and half-heartedly tries various diets in a good humoured way. She shouldn't compare herself to most of the rest of us who are naturally skinny. The food is edible, but I can't wait for someone to ask me out for a proper meal.

Oh yes, the dreaded tests. Well I've worked out that I can get zero for the last two and still end up with over 50 per cent. So I'm in, hoorah!

Clean, shiny, stainless steel and warm from the heated rack, bedpans were a world away from the cardboard creations of today. The bedpan round was a regular part of the ward routine. Patients were offered them on waking, before or after meals and visiting hours. The pans were loaded onto a trolley and tactfully covered with thin paper bags which were ideal for jotting names on as often the contents had to be measured, tested or collected. After bowel motions the patients were given a bowl of warm water, soap and a towel to wash their hands. Usually several nurses would help with the round, pulling curtains and helping patients on and off, and, if necessary, changing the draw sheet (a narrow sheet placed horizontally on the bed on top of a waterproof layer and under the patient's bottom that could be changed quickly and easily if there was an 'accident'). But, of course, it was the junior's job to dispose of the contents down the sluice, scrub the pans and sterilise them one at a time in a noisy machine, and remove them seconds later when they were too hot to handle without a handy thick cloth for protection. As junior nurses we were soon Queens of the Sluice; it was the room where we felt confident and safest. It was our domain and we took pride in keeping it scrupulously clean and tidy. We secured the full bags of rubbish or dirty linen, lugged them to the chutes and flung them on their way. We soon learnt that the occasional flood was most easily mopped up by grabbing towels out of the dirty laundry bag and using them to soak up the worst of it, a skill that remains with me for life! The sluice, or the linen cupboard, was also a private space for the occasional, but inevitable, tears.

The juniors started the day serving breakfasts (after carefully checking which patients were 'Nil by Mouth'). We learnt to be observant to the needs of the patients, as some used a feeder cup with a spout because they couldn't manage a cup and saucer, and others needed help with feeding. The bedpan round followed once breakfast was cleared away, and then the next job was 'sides'. This involved damp dusting the patients' lockers and over-bed tables, replacing the white paper bag for rubbish which was taped to the locker and refreshing the water jugs and glasses. Nowadays this is considered a menial task that a cleaner on a lower wage could easily perform, whereas we were taught that it was not only essential hygiene, but a chance to chat and get to know the patients. Whilst we were busy cleaning, they would often share their fears with us about their condition or problems at home, which could be relayed to Sister and she could tackle the issues when she did her ward round, speaking to every patient, later in the morning. Sides was an opportunity to form a relationship with the patient as a person so they became more than a name and diagnosis, and a task most of us enjoyed. We were expected to know every patient by name (more than thirty of them on most wards) and to be familiar with their condition and treatment, even though this meant updating our knowledge every shift.

Mornings were a busy time as everyone had to have a good wash. This could involve help to the bathroom, help with washing in bed or a complete bed bath, including brushing hair and teeth, for seriously ill or post-operative patients. Sometimes on the bigger wards, or if we were short staffed, this could be a real race against the clock, but somehow by lunchtime everyone was clean and the beds had been remade with a clean top sheet, (yesterday's top sheet became the bottom) and clean pillow cases.

During the afternoon visiting hour we would remove all the flowers, discard the dying ones and arrange new bunches in vases. We were paranoid about not placing only red and white flowers together (this superstition comes from blood and bandages, barbers performing surgery, and signifies death). A surprising number of visitors were unaware of this and we quietly re-jigged arrangements, never said a word, and no one appeared to notice the vase of flowers on their locker was not quite the same as the bunch they were given! We took all the flowers out at night and replaced them in the morning. To this day I hate to see half-dead flowers left unattended and I never put only red and white flowers together. Sadly flowers are no longer allowed in most hospitals.

The women's wards used to smell lovely with the perfumes of talcum powder and scented soap. The men generously shared their fruit and chocolates with the nurses and all the patients appreciated the colourful floral arrangements surrounded by Get Well cards on their lockers. They gave everybody's spirits a lift and softened the clinical severity of the wards. The convalescent patients (for there was such a thing then) would assist with coffee, tea and evening drink rounds, and also changing water jugs and flowers. This was encouraged as light physical and occupational therapy for them and provided invaluable help to the nurses.

Letters home:

23rd October 1967

Tuesday afternoon we were on a B shift. I did all the usual things like bedpans, rubbing backs to prevent pressure sores and making beds. Also I took a patient to X-ray all by myself, and was promoted to giving post-operative care unsupervised. I was terrified that I'd forget something, but I don't think I did. Coming off duty I felt so tired and my feet and legs ached because we'd been busy and missed our tea break as we were short-staffed. Sister wasn't there, but to my horror our sister tutor appeared unexpectedly. She left again after about five minutes, during which time I walked around looking madly efficient and made a show of washing my hands thoroughly because I didn't have a clue what I was supposed to be doing next!

I've bought the new blouse; it is white lace, with a high collar and leg of mutton sleeves. It makes me feel all feminine and flirty, and yet it looks staid too. Does that make sense? It cost £4, a fortune on my salary, but it is worth every penny. I've made myself a black velvet drawstring evening bag, with offcuts from the skirt, to enhance the Edwardian image. Sweet and demure, that's me.

Wednesday we were back in the jolly old school room still suffering from the effects of the previous day's work. That evening I went round to Robert's digs. We sat and talked for a bit and then went to the cinema to see The Knack, which was hilarious but a bit crude in places, and I wasn't sure if it was ladylike to laugh. He's got a good sense of humour and is fun to be with.

Thursday brought the last test of PTS, welcome news for me but terrifying for several of the girls. Now the results are in the bag, but Gill and I know we are definitely through with an average of 74 per cent at the moment.

On Friday morning, I did it! I bed bathed a man, and I was in charge of mouth care and took blood pressures too. The afternoon dragged unbelievably slowly. The lecture was so boring and we thought it would never be tea time when we could start preparing for the ball. It took five hours, but I was ready and waiting when Patrick arrived at 9.30pm, looking very dashing in his dinner jacket. Even better, Gill has a driving licence and she had persuaded her mother to lend her the mini for the evening. She chauffeured us to the Dorothy Café in great style.

Did it really take us five hours to get ready? The anticipation of our first Cambridge Ball pushed excitement levels to fever pitch as those of us with tickets flitted along the corridors, taking turns in the bathrooms and visiting each other to borrow things and check on progress. We wandered around in our dressing gowns with rollers in our hair, experimented with new make-up and debated the choice of colour for nail varnish. The corridor echoed with fits of giggles, exclamations of admiration and joy, and the occasional squeal of anguish accompanied by a cry for help. Everyone joined in the preparations, even those that weren't going to the ball. I left brushing my hair out until last. I had a picture in my head of how I wanted it to look and was delighted when the top back-combed efficiently and the sides swept back beautifully. As I removed the rollers the ringlets cascaded over my shoulders perfectly, and I fastened an artificial corsage of marguerites, borrowed from my mother, to cover the hair grips.

I climbed carefully into my new blouse and skirt and slipped on my slightly scuffed black patent shoes, wishing I could have afforded a new pair. I picked up the velvet bag and admired myself in the mirror. I had created the effect I wanted and was ready to dance the night away.

The Dorothy Café was not, as you might imagine, a tearoom. You have to think more Café Royal on Regent Street in London to get a clearer image of the perfect venue for a ball. It was the very place my parents had first met many years earlier, and now I was about to go through the door. (It has since been redeveloped and is now a huge book store.) As we entered and mounted the long flight of stairs, we looked up to see Matron, in her evening gown, at the top. She shook hands with each of us, with a formal courtesy which felt curiously as if she was welcoming us into her home as part of her family. My eyes darted hither and thither as I exclaimed over the magnificent rooms and the extravagant floral arrangements, and I know Patrick was impressed too. I gazed enviously at some of the elaborate ballgowns and smothered giggles over the more outlandish outfits. With a thrill I realised this was Cambridge, where you either conform in style or rebel with bohemian eccentricity, and both are equally acceptable.

Curiosity soon urged us to explore, and we peeped into the Blue Room where we found a Jazz Band and a bar. Drinks in hand, we wandered on to the Oak Room, suitably panelled and dimly lit, which housed a discotheque with a hippy girl playing familiar romantic records. The atmosphere was ideal for slow smoochy dancing and a few couples were already wrapped around each other, making the most of the opportunity. But not us, oh no! I was much too excited and impatiently moved Patrick quickly on. We found ourselves in a huge ornate room with chandeliers, a real ballroom with a sprung floor. For a moment all I could do was stare and try to convince myself that this was true and it really was me standing there, for it seemed to be straight out of a fairy tale. The waltz finished to a smattering of polite applause and the band swung effortlessly into a Glenn

Miller tune for a quickstep. As always I wished I had a boyfriend who knew how to dance properly, but I encouraged Patrick to try and did my best to keep my feet out from under his as I propelled him determinedly round the edges of the dance floor. Later a Latin American group took centre stage, playing catchy tunes. The foot-tapping rhythms caused everyone to join in; the floor was crowded, couples bumped into each other, laughing good naturedly, and everyone had fantastic fun. Out of breath and feeling peckish, we went in search of food only to discover there was a turkey buffet and coffee, but for an extra charge of 13 shillings per couple, which neither of us could afford. Fortunately water was free. Refreshed and ready to join in again, we were swept up in a long conga line that was collecting couples from all the rooms and heading back to the ballroom. This turned out to be the beginning of the grand finale; the conga line eventually formed a circle and we all danced the 'Hokey Cokey', followed by 'Knees Up Mother Brown' and the 'Lambeth Walk'. We were so exhilarated we could have danced all night. Instead we crossed arms, joined hands and sang 'Auld Lang Syne' enthusiastically. As the singing died away, the mood changed to quiet acceptance whilst the band played the 'Last Waltz' and couples came close and wished time would stand still. It didn't; our first Cambridge Ball was over.

The ball went on until 3am. We had such a wonderful time. Patrick walked me home. We said good-night in the park and then parted politely at the door of Owlstonecroft under Home Sister's ever watchful eye! I felt very emotional and I ran to my room and wept tears of happiness all over Gill. (We do seem to spend a lot of time crying on each other's shoulders.)

On Saturday morning Gill woke me because her brother and his friend were taking us to the Newmarket Races. It rained and we got soaked, but all found it amusing huddled together under one umbrella. We couldn't afford to place real bets, but had fun guessing which horses would win. In the evening, in dry clothes, we ate at the Corner House, had a drink at The Fountain and then went to the cinema to see Grand Prix which was the boys' choice. It was horribly noisy and so lifelike you could almost smell the petrol. It was midnight before I got to bed, tired but happy.

Sunday morning Gill and I went to Matins at the Round Church. The church was packed and everyone joined in the hymns, but the sermon was like a bible study and went on for half an hour. Lunch at Owlstonecroft was disgusting, but it didn't matter as we'd been invited for tea at Jesus College. We ate crumpets, chocolate cake, biscuits and somebody's twenty-first birthday cake too. Even better, they've invited us again next Thursday. We left after sherry, not my favourite tipple, and I met Robert for a drink at The Castle. I'm seeing him again next Tuesday. As you can see, Gill and I are doing our best to get to know as many undergrads as possible: all types, all sorts, and lots of new experiences, of the cleanest kind I hasten to assure you!

STOP PRESS NEWS: I saw Prince Charles walking down Lensfield Road with a man, presumably his detective. It didn't really click it was him until I had cycled past, and then it registered: my goodness, Prince Charles!

Once again it was midnight before I was asleep, and today, Monday, I am dog-tired, and to crown it all we had a practical session this morning. One of the others took my observations with the following worryingly accurate results: Temp. 100F, Pulse 98, BP 90/60 and my glands are up. What is going on? I don't feel ill, but it doesn't look good. I shall have a bath and go to bed early tonight just in case.

We got our little chat on sex this morning. Didn't teach me anything new, but I was amazed how naive some of the others are. We got the inevitable warning about boyfriends, drugs and excess of alcohol. Then an interesting prediction that by the end of training at least two of us would be married, most of us engaged, and at least two pregnant with illegitimate babies. I thought they were pretty encouraging odds!

We get next weekend off, and then we are on the wards forever and ever, so I'll probably come home whilst I can. Must dash now as this boring lecture is coming to an end and I want to post this on the way to tea.

Despite my joking about sex, I should explain that society in general still frowned upon sex before marriage, and getting pregnant meant total disgrace for both the girl and her family. This was still an era when contraception was not readily available and pregnant girls were forced into 'shot-gun' weddings, or hidden away in homes for 'fallen women' and had to give up their illegitimate children for adoption. Bastard was an ugly word. Attitudes slowly changed, but it wasn't until 1973 that a benefit was introduced enabling a mother to keep her illegitimate child and the expression 'single mother' was first used.

31st October 1967

First of all the breaking news: I'm in Sick Bay at the Old Site. I've got glandular fever; nothing common like tonsillitis. I'm stuck here, and none of my friends are allowed to visit in case they catch it. Is everybody happy? You bet your life I'm not. At times it gets very lonely, and I feel rotten with a temperature that keeps rocketing skywards and a throat that is slowly throttling me. I've felt homesick for the first time, partly because they are talking of moving me to Brookfields, the isolation hospital. I've been signed off for at least two weeks. Gill has been an absolute brick and volunteered to bring in things I need and wash my nighties, what a pal. Liz, Angie and some of the others write funny notes to cheer me up. The nurses working on Thomas Potter Ward look after us, trot in and out and stop to chat whenever possible. Another nurse has glandular fever too and was admitted on the same day.

Much more exciting is I came second in our set with 77 per cent. The girl who beat me was going to be a medic, but changed her mind. I feel very clever and exceptionally lucky as it seems criminal to do so little work and get good marks. For that last test I got 24/25, a flourishing finish, eh? When I get back to work I'll be able to wear my belt over my apron, hoorah! Unfortunately nine girls have to leave us, but most of them are going to move to smaller hospitals to continue training and that will probably suit them better. I was quite glad to be up here away from the floods of tears.

I am beginning to suspect Dracula lives in the Haematology Department. He's had three lots of my blood already. The swab of pus from my throat didn't grow any bugs, most likely because they are still here killing me, and they haven't said a thing about my beautiful mid-stream urine specimen. I can see my effort was quite unappreciated. I am confined to my room and I have to use bedpans, it's hilarious. I find it embarrassing being asked if I've had a bowel motion when I haven't eaten anything more solid than an egg for a week. Short pause whilst I drink a glass of 'something' which has to be done at increasingly regular intervals to keep my fluids up and is awful as it hurts so much to swallow.

Oh my goodness, guess who just came in to see me? Matron! Talk about a shock, someone might have warned me. Actually she is wonderful, exchanged a few sentences, asked if there was anything I wanted and patted my legs before doing an exodus with a wink. She is very human and everyone loves her; you can't help it.

I must point out that although I was tired, I was not run down. I have not been overly swotting as the doc seems to think. Gill could tell them I haven't done a stroke of work since the third week and very little before then. I've only used late passes at weekends and often not even then. Personally I consider I was only normally tired after a hectic weekend and would have been fine again in a couple of days if this bug hadn't hit me. If everyone else's theory that I was overworked, overtired and rundown is true then no doubt this will reoccur (I sincerely hope not) and I shall have to seriously consider that I may not be tough enough for nursing. I dread that possibility and hope time will prove otherwise.

I've written to Patrick saying I won't see him anymore. The ball made him think we are a couple and I just don't feel like that about him. I'm sorry if I have hurt him, but I just can't cope with a serious boyfriend at the moment. It seemed best, if rather harsh, to be honest.

6th November 1967

The doc saw me today. Apparently my liver is misbehaving which explains why I was decidedly yellow, but it is not infectious hepatitis so I can stay here. I've been moved to a bigger room with a TV set, but I can only get BBC1. The advantage of being stuck in bed is I can buzz for a bedpan and not miss any of the film on TV, ideal really. It was a bit embarrassing when my period started and I had to ask for some sanitary towels, but I guess the experience will help me understand how patients feel when I'm back on the wards. It's all a bit undignified. My friends are jealous because I can watch Magic Roundabout every evening. It is the funniest programme, especially the parting comment, which is usually completely out of context and madly ambiguous. I think I should stop watching the News as it makes my blood boil and that can't do me any good. Why is our pompous Government so stupid? I shan't vote for them when I get to twenty-one.

At the moment I am reading Gone with the Wind and in two days have got a third of the way through, despite falling asleep at regular intervals. I've completed the back and both sleeves of my jumper. At this rate I'll have finished it before they let me out.

22nd November 1967

This is a short letter as I've not got much news and Mother can bring it home to save me the postage. I do love her visits: she cheers me up no end. The Chaplain popped in and we had a long chat about drama, acting and the theatre in general. It made me realise how privileged I am to have been to see lots of plays, something I've rather taken for granted. He never mentioned God or the Church once.

The girl next door is up and around and going home on Friday. Meanwhile I am still stuck in bed until my liver function returns to normal, so I guess I'll be here for a while yet. Trust me to be an interesting case; it's not fair as I've been the perfect patient. I'll try and make it home for my birthday, ever the optimist!

Addenbrooke's Hospital
5th December 1967

Dear Mrs Walker,

I was sorry to miss seeing you when you came to fetch Eileen yesterday. I think that she will now make rapid strides and we shall look forward to having her back in due course, but not until she is really fit to return. She has been a wonderful patient and I told her I think she will make a very good nurse, so we look forward to her future with pleasure.

Yours sincerely,
M.M. Puddicombe
Matron.

I did get home for my birthday, and for the School Leavers' Prize Giving Ceremony. I had been seriously ill and my liver, although functioning normally again, was still fragile, which meant a ban on alcohol for the next twelve months. Convalescence was a slow process because I was very weak after six weeks in bed and still kept falling asleep during the day. It was hard to pull myself out of the invalid mentality and push myself to stay awake and improve my physical fitness. I was suffering from what is now called Post Viral Fatigue. During my absence our set had moved from the extension into the main building at Owlstonecroft. Our new rooms were on the third, the top, floor. Mine was immediately opposite the lift and above the main door (easily spotted from outside as the one with Busy

Lizzies on the windowsill). Gill was still next door, and Liz and Angie were along the corridor and around the corner. The lift was noisy and the outer wooden door banged loudly, which Gill found infuriating when she was on night duty and trying to sleep. She took to sticking notices up on the inside of the lift door imploring the other nurses to shut it quietly. When my turn for night duty came it was not a problem; I could sleep through anything.

In the New Year I was determined to get back to work, but this was daunting as I knew I had missed a lot of practical nursing experience and would be starting my first ward when my friends were moving on to their second. Somehow I had to catch up.

First Year

Letters to All at Home:

16th January 1968

Working on the usual assumption that if I want to receive some letters then I'd better write one, I'm writing!

I was greeted with "Hello, Eileen, are you back?", a stupid question from all and sundry, but I was welcomed with open arms on Ward 4, which has been seriously understaffed.

On Monday I worked an A shift which almost finished me off, I was exhausted. Of course there is a completely new set of patients and I've had to learn their names, as well as what is wrong with them. One lady is mad as a hatter, my first experience of dementia, and keeps determinedly setting off out of the ward in her nightie and slippers, clutching her handbag. She is convinced there is nothing wrong with her (so why is her arm in plaster?) and won't co-operate unless she feels like it. It's a full time occupation trying to keep her in her bed, or her chair, and out of the other patients' lockers. In contrast there is a lovely old man who has First World War shrapnel scars that he is forever telling me about, though he is actually here because he fractured his femur. He likes the young nurses and is often rude about the others, making it hard to keep a straight face.

Today I was on a split shift, but guess who overslept? And guess who had arranged for two people to call for her on their way to breakfast, and they both forgot? And guess who was two hours late on duty, had to pay for a taxi and got torn off a strip by one of the Assistant Matrons? I nearly cried.

I thought I'd safe-guarded being late by asking friends to check I was up, and how was I to know that I was supposed to kneel at the Assistant Matron's feet and apologise? She said it was grossly impolite of me, and I felt tempted to smile sweetly and say I was terribly sorry, but as I had never been late before I hadn't known what was expected in the circumstances. Instead I bit my tongue, begged her pardon, and she graciously said I had better make the time up and work until two o'clock. Luckily everyone on Ward 4 was very kind, and Staff Nurse sent me to eat at 1.30pm, otherwise I would have missed lunch altogether. This evening Sister will be on, which is a bit scary, but I'm picking things up fairly quickly, and as we are bound to be busy, it won't be too hard to keep out of her way.

Our ward goes onto internal rotation soon, but they won't let me do nights until my second ward. It's a new system that means you do a stint of night duty on each ward instead of the old long block of nights on only one or two wards. It makes sense as we will get to experience all twenty-four hours on every ward. Personally I'd like to do some nights as it is quieter and there is time to read the patients' notes and find out more about them; on days there is no chance as we are busy caring for them all the time.

20th January 1968

For my first injection I had to give intramuscular Pethidine and I managed with a beautifully steady hand. Mind you, I was shaking like a leaf afterwards. I've also been trusted with urine testing, but that is hardly so exciting. Sister is being very considerate and gives me the children to look after, which I love.

I took one of them down to have a plaster cast applied, encasing one leg and the whole trunk to immobilise the hip joint. I found it a fascinating procedure to watch. The doctors use bandages with lots of flakes of Plaster of Paris in the gauze which are soaked in water and applied exactly like a bandage, except over stockingette to protect the skin, and they build up several layers. Then they turn back the ends of the stockingette and give it one more layer, smoothing the plaster with the hands, and the cast hardens as it dries.

Today I watched Staff Nurse dress a leg stump following an amputation for gangrene in a diabetic patient. She says I can do the dressing next time and she'll watch. I succeeded in getting one cantankerous old lady to drink her fluids without a murmur, and I managed to bath our mad as a hatter patient which was no mean feat. She stank because she'd been wetting herself. I soon discovered the thing to do was to play along with her, even if it did mean getting some funny looks from Sister. We went to the bathroom to 'feed the ducks' and I suggested she got in for a little splash about. In the process I got a bit wet, but she was clean, smelled sweet, and even had her hair washed. It was a minor triumph (especially as I managed to keep the plaster cast on her arm dry) and I felt very proud when Sister said, "Well done".

The Cambridge grapevine is working true to form, and within three days Robert knew I was back, though how I don't know. He took me to see two films: Far from the Madding Crowd, which brings the book to life quite brilliantly, and Dr Faustus, which I can't say much about as I dozed through most of it! Gill gets back soon. I'll be pleased to see her as most of the others are on holiday and I am missing Gill's understanding and companionship. Doubtless I shall hear all about the marvellous time she has had seeing Henry again. I can't wait to meet him as according to Gill no one in Cambridge is half as wonderful. Henry must be fantastic!

29th January 1968

I am discovering nursing can be a lonely job. You meet lots of people in passing, but it is difficult to get to know anyone properly. One would think that with the great surplus of males in Cambridge it would be easy to make stacks of friends, but oh no. Each boy wants you for himself, and if you think you are going to have fun meeting his friends, you're mistaken. You just get chatting and he turns up to whisk you away again, possessive or what? How did you guess? Robert is getting too keen and is pushing for more than just friends. Men!

I am enjoying the ward work which has been slack as Ward 3 has been taking all the admissions. Suddenly yesterday all our beds filled, and it will be hectic tomorrow. Any minute I might get my first death as we have two patients dying from cancer. I got a bit of a shock when I realised this. Once cancer has spread to the bones; the patients need pain control, but as long as we get that right, they don't look as ill as I imagined they would, just thin and worn out. It makes me more determined to keep them as comfortable as possible and care for them as well as I can. Nurses say "Lots of TLC", which stands for Tender Loving Care.

My exciting social life continues. I've been to another party, but am getting fed up with being teased for only drinking orange juice and having to keep explaining about my liver. It was more interesting going to see How I Won the War, a clever new film that parodies the fiasco of the First World War. It was very funny, but sad too; difficult to explain, you have to go and see it. The next night we saw Twelfth Night at the Arts Theatre. Afterwards there was an amusing incident on the way home when a policeman stopped me.

"And what's happened to your lights, my girl?"

"Lights?" I said, all sweet and innocent. "Oh I must have forgotten to switch the dynamo on, I'm terribly sorry".

Sure enough, the dynamo was not on the wheel, and he moved it and said, "You want to be more careful, my girl."

Surprise, surprise, we then discovered neither of my lights worked anyway and he insisted on walking me back to the Nurses' Home, and chatted me up on the way! I suppose I ought to get them fixed.

No one else has the same day off as me. If Mother could

come over it would be fun to go shopping. It's taken four trips to the finance office, but I should have some money to spend by then: happy thought as I have my October salary, sick pay and January's pay to come. I shall be rich. I could buy you lunch.

There were new experiences every day on Ward 4. We were often short staffed, but this was to my advantage as I was given more opportunities and greater responsibility sooner. It was a fast learning curve, but I felt more confident as I got to know the patients and their little ways. In no time I understood the routine, what I was supposed to be doing, and knew where everything was kept. I enjoyed being part of a team and joining in the back-chat that is so typical of nurses. I became efficient at giving injections and nasogastric feeds, tackled the joys of suppositories and enemas, and acquired the skills of pre- and post-operative care. I was even allowed to do some of the more straightforward dressings. I realised how much progress I had made when the new PTS set came to the ward for their first day and I was asked to show them how to do things, a huge boost to my morale.

Sadly I was still not back to optimum health. The long shifts, combined with always being on our feet and busy, left me exhausted and ready for lovely long luxurious baths. My social life was limited to the evenings before a lie-in to ensure I did not get overtired. Even so I had to have a couple of days off sick with tonsillitis, which had been a regular occurrence throughout my childhood. Everyone, including Sister, was delighted to see me back on the ward, and the patients said they had missed me, but that could be taken two ways!

20th February 1968

Today we admitted a new patient following a messy road traffic accident. He has fractured both femurs, shattered his left tibia, broken his right arm, has lacerations everywhere and concussion. I've been looking after him all by myself and felt chuffed to be trusted.

There is another super new patient; he's nineteen and the most fantastic hunk of male flesh that I've seen for ages. Fortunately I've a head start on the other nurses as I met him, with his parents, on Accident Service before he came up to the ward. Sadly he only has a fractured fibula and will be out again on crutches in a couple of days.

What, you may be wondering, was I doing in Accident Service? Well, don't laugh: guess who got a fish bone stuck in her throat! Would it swallow down? No. Was I sick? Yes. Did it come up? No. It was firmly stuck so I had to go to have it removed. As you can imagine, a nurse, in uniform, as a patient caused quite a stir. Whilst I was waiting, and feeling more and more embarrassed, who should turn up but the doctor who is heart-throb of the hospital! He thought it was hilarious and said it served me right for eating hospital food. Then he got a bit concerned as it was so far down it was difficult to see and he wasn't sure the long forceps could reach it. I said determinedly that I was sure he'd manage. When his handsome face leant very close to mine it was rather disconcerting, but that distracted me from the ordeal and he fished it out. (Excuse the pun.) He said I owe him a drink, and another doctor said I'd be a lot less chatty if they'd removed my throat! It was a bit of an anticlimax to have to go back to the ward and I had to put up with a lot of good natured teasing, but I rather enjoyed that.

We're going to see Pirates of Penzance tomorrow night at the Arts Theatre if we can get in free. Did you see Prof Barnard, the South African heart transplant surgeon, and our Prof Calne on television talking about organ transplants? We all watched and were thrilled to see Addenbrooke's Hospital Kidney Unit featured.

28th February 1968

The January set, below us, have fallen on their feet pretty quickly. They had to because yesterday we only had one senior, myself and the new girl on duty, and a long theatre list

42

which occupied all the senior's time and left me to organise the rest of the ward. I guess the poor girl has never worked so hard in all her life, but we managed to get everything done between us.

Monday night we went to see No Man's Land at the Arts Theatre. Usually it is the most expensive tickets that haven't been sold and we get to sit in the best seats absolutely free. You know how much I adore watching plays and I know we are very lucky to have the chance to see so many new productions. It is easy to think this is normal, especially after all those times I got tickets for the Mermaid Theatre in Blackfriars when I was in the sixth form as part payment for babysitting. All in all I've been thoroughly spoilt the last few years. I prefer the Art's Theatre as it is more traditional. I do love the magic of the curtains opening and the anticipation of wondering what the set is like. It is fabulous to settle into the comfy seat, watch the lights dim and be transported into another world, far away from bedpans and aching feet... even if it is to the trenches in the Great War!

On the way home I bumped, almost literally, into a friend from Brentwood School (the one that played the male lead in our sixth form drama production). I walked as far as Corpus Christi College with him and then had to cycle the rest of the way back in two minutes flat so as to be home before the curfew. I just made it; Home Sister was on the doorstep watching the clock. I must dash now and change into uniform. What a life; it's all go, but I wouldn't change it for the world.

3rd March 1968

This is a short note to let you know I am in the land of the living, even if I look like death warmed up, as people keep telling me, and the sister tutor is convinced I'm anorexic! I feel fine, though I am more than ready for a holiday. I've had a letter from our super patient (tall, dark and handsome) asking me out. The others are madly jealous, especially as he's the nicest person I've met in a long time.

Work was challenging on Saturday when I was sent down to help on Accident Service.

"They are very busy and I'm afraid you'll have to go and help."

"Me? Shouldn't it be someone more senior?"

"Yes, but I can't spare the senior so it will have to be you."

Down I went in fear and trembling as we are supposed to be well into our second year before we go near Accident Service. Fortunately everything was fairly routine and easy once I'd got the hang of it. Mind you, for what seemed like ages the other two nurses had to be in theatre and I was left holding the fort, terrified in case the emergency red telephone rang and I had to answer it. Thank God it didn't.

Back on the ward we've got five children, which is great fun. The maid had highly polished the long corridor floor and the seven-year-old boy asked me to push his wheelchair as fast as I could up the length of it. So off we went until I was running flat out, then I let my feet slide and we stopped just before we hit the ward doors. In the thrill of the moment I rather forgot that nurses must never run. For a few minutes I didn't feel like a nurse at all and now I go cold thinking what might have happened if it had all gone wrong. If he mentions it to Sister, she'll kill me.

I've got some work to get finished and handed in before Yellow Block, but that is not a problem. I'm looking forward to coming home Saturday afternoon.

After PTS, nurses learnt by experience on the wards with instruction from their seniors, but every so often there was a study block of four weeks when we returned to the classroom for lectures and teaching sessions. The blocks were called by colour: yellow, green, red and blue. During block we had evenings and weekends off, but were expected to study in our spare time.

Yellow Block got off to a bad start. We had a sister tutor

who seemed to have lost the plot, going over digestion instead of nutrition and spending most of the time reminiscing about the Second World War. The whole set was fed up. Gill and I were persuaded, as their representatives, to talk to the Principle Tutor. As a result that sister tutor was asked to retire gracefully and we got an excellent replacement. Inevitably some of our colleagues then accused us of engineering her downfall, saying it was a mean and nasty thing to do, which we both found hurtful. Despite this, the glorious weather soon lifted our spirits as we cycled along The Backs, admiring the abundant crocuses, daffodils and the willow trees wearing their new green. Cambridge is even more beautiful in the spring. We sunbathed, played tennis and went to watch Charlie Girl at the theatre, enjoying the regular hours and the company of our friends. The days flew by as we relaxed into being schoolgirls again with no responsibilities. When Cambridge won the Boat Race our cheers shook the walls of the television lounge, but we came back to earth when Home Sister promptly decided to check all the hospital markings on our bedding. This meant we had to strip and remake our beds two days running as the usual fortnightly change of laundry was the previous day. Revision for the end of block test added to our woes, and the general assumption that I would come top put me under unnecessary pressure. I was apprehensive about seeing Matron to discuss my first ward report on the last day, but it went well, and I was delighted to get my first year belt with all the others, even though I had less ward experience. Then I escaped home on holiday, exhausted but with my mouth watering at the thought of home cooking.

Addenbrooke's Hospital

Dear Mrs Walker,

I am pleased to tell you that Eileen has successfully completed her period of trial duties and I have told her that I am ready to recommend her to the committee for training here.

She has entered into an understanding with me concerning

this, the period of training being three years and three months, in which the Introductory Course is included.

I am so glad that your daughter has settled down happily with us and I hope a very successful career lies before her.

Yours sincerely,

M.M. Puddicombe

Matron.

3rd May 1968

Most people don't write letters at three o'clock in the morning, but nurses do. I love nights, it's super. I'm working at the Old Site now and we all have to queue up outside Night Sister's office to clock on, which gives us a chance to see who else is on duty and creates a feeling of camaraderie as we take over the hospital for the night. It's great, completely different from days as there is less to do once the patients are all settled, apart from paperwork, tidying up, the odd bedpan, drugs and observations. It is very peaceful sitting knitting in our little pool of light whilst all around us are asleep. We have an hour for supper and a half hour coffee break. My senior sleeps in her break and it is a bit scary being in charge, but the bonus is I get to sit in Sister's chair. The ward sisters have wooden, old and well worn Windsor chairs which are incredibly comfortable. I'd love to have one of my own. I find I don't need to nap during the night as I sleep well during the day, and even have to get someone to wake me up to ensure I'm not late on duty. If my friends come up during the break we go in the office, but still have to talk in whispers and smother the laughs so as not to disturb the patients. We drink gallons of coffee and get exercise traipsing across the hospital and up all the stairs to the top floor to get the theatre list. We are not allowed to use the lifts here at night as they make too much noise. Everyone is much friendlier and I fail to understand why so many nurses claim to hate night duty. I love it.

I'm lucky to be working on Goode (gynaecology) which

is a smaller ward and relatively quiet. Whilst on day duty I learnt lots of new things: how to catheterise women, help with drug rounds and take out the clips that are often used now instead of stitches. I've seen a colostomy and am a dab hand at shaves, enemas and vaginal irrigation. Unfortunately I did make one minor mistake and Sister was on my case. I don't object to being told off once, but I hate being treated as a complete idiot from that moment on. You'll be pleased to know I had sorted it anyway before she found out and there was no harm done. Why make so much petty fuss? She hasn't done the off duty rota for next week yet either.

That's the thing I dislike about nursing: there is too much pettiness and muddled priorities and not enough co-operation. I'm glad to be on night duty now and away from all that; hopefully by next week she'll have forgotten about it. My senior on nights is super and the night sisters are great; well, all except one (who is a bit of a stickler and expects to find you reading notes and not knitting), but we usually get a phone call warning she is on her way up. The senior was telling me that it used to be a lot busier on nights when the nurses had to pack swabs and do the sterilising. She says I should be forever grateful for CSSD (Central Sterile Supplies Department) and never take it for granted. They are responsible for all that work now, and we have sterile packs to hand and simply send them the used forceps and unused swabs to sort out. We use plastic syringes and needles that are disposable too. We think we are hard worked, but I guess we are luckier than we realise when we have time to knit and write letters.

There is an air of excitement in the hospital. News has leaked out that the first ever liver transplant was done by Prof Calne at Douglas House yesterday afternoon. No doubt it will be in all the papers soon, but it is thrilling that it happened here at Addenbrooke's and we are the first people to know. I wonder how successful it will be.

I've been to the theatre twice. We saw Emma and then Sybil Thorndyke in Night Must Fall – I had to pay for that one. She was brilliant; fantastic to see a professional performance so soon after our amateur effort in the sixth form. We watched Charge of the Light Brigade at the cinema too, very dramatic.

Now I'm on nights again and it has been very quiet. My senior is a great laugh and has me in hysterics. It's a miracle we don't wake the patients. I'm sleeping well despite all the glorious weather and am glad I don't have to resort to sleeping tablets like some of the others.

We've got a patient in having treatment for cancer of the cervix which means her vagina is packed with radium. She is nursed in a side ward (a single room off the main ward) because of the radiation and we all have to wear little badges pinned to our waists to check we are not over exposed. The Chaplain jokes that he is the only person who doesn't wear one, and yet he sits with her for long chats and we mostly flit in and out. I get the impression there is no guarantee this treatment will work in the sense of a cure, but I guess even if it buys her a bit more time it is worth it as her children are only teenagers.

20th June 1968

I am writing this on Eye Ward. I'm relieving here during the other nurse's break, which is a bit frightening because I don't know the first thing about eyes. The floorboards creak and everyone is asleep as they are not ill, strictly speaking. I've been told that at any moment the phone might ring and I'd have to start getting the eye theatre ready for an emergency operation; quite how I don't know either, and there is no one to ask.

A nurse popped in to see me from the Blue Room: that's the three bed, sometimes more, intensive care unit and is next door. (There is often a patient suffering from tetanus in there as it is easily caught from the East Anglia soil. The patient has to be paralysed by drugs and artificially ventilated until the bug has burnt out. Can you imagine being completely paralysed and unable to communicate, but fully conscious, for weeks on end? Horrid!) The nurse asked if she could have a white flower to place in the hands of a young child who has just died of pneumonia so he looks angelic when his parents see him. Apparently that is a thoughtful touch that is always added for children, and I thought it was such a lovely gesture. I'm sure the eye patient won't notice one flower has disappeared.

Earlier this week I relieved on Victoria (women's surgical) which was interesting. One of the patients is in for tests prior to possibly doing a liver transplant. I took the opportunity to read all her notes and, as she was awake, made her a cuppa and had a chat. So maybe I've met the second ever person who will have a liver transplant.

Goode was exceptionally quiet this week because the beds were slowly emptying before a huge bulk of admissions today, twelve of them, as it is the medics' exams this weekend. That means four major operations on Friday, seven more on Saturday and the rest on Monday. It'll be a hectic time. Luckily I leave at the crucial moment, because although Saturday night will be hell, and we probably won't get a break at all, I shall keep going by thinking of my nights off. The patients are a cheerful bunch, which helps.

Working with a different senior has been a terrific strain. I spend all my time trying not to argue with her, calming down the patients she has upset and checking that all the senior jobs have been done as well as all my own. I seriously hope she fails her finals because she is a hopeless nurse.

Liz and Angie are on nights too, and Gill comes on this Saturday. It was fantastic the other morning as the four of us were all off duty together for practically the first time in history. We sat on the floor of the top corridor and talked about moving out. We have decided to rent a flat together, and now all we have to do is find it. We're going to see the nurses' social advisor next week as apparently she will help and knows all the snags. Gill is thrilled she's been moved to Children's Ward unexpectedly; she loves the children, especially the babies (another thing we have in common), and is thoroughly enjoying it. With a bit of luck we'll get to be on nights together more often. I've only seen her for three hours this week, and that's a record. Talking of records, I am delighted with my record player. I know it was expensive, but it is brilliant to be able to listen to music of my choice, and my collection of LPs is growing.

4th July 1968

Poor old Gill has got chickenpox. Fortunately she was at her parents' house when the spots came out. At this rate she'll have had as much time off sick as me, if that's possible.

We both missed all the fun and games here at Owlstonecroft whilst we were away on nights off. You know where my room is on the third floor? Well the girl next door is in the corner room, and her boyfriend is well known as one of the night climbers of Cambridge. He's very experienced and skilled and has climbed King's College Chapel, onto the Senate House roof and either in or out of most of the colleges during the night when they are all locked and secure. Someone challenged him to climb into my neighbour's room, quite a task because this place is like Fort Knox. Apparently he managed it, but only because she leant out and gave him a hand to climb around the opened casement window from the drainpipe. After the euphoria of success had worn off, they realised this procedure would be impossible in reverse and decided to creep down to the first floor and he could get out through the bedroom window of a nurse they thought was on night duty. They were wrong. She awoke in the dark to find a strange man in her room and ran, screaming blue murder, straight to Home Sister. She's a bit straight-laced and part of the God Squad. By the time the boyfriend decided to climb out of the window anyway, the police were there with open arms to catch him. Home Sister was on the warpath, trying to identify the culprits, but everyone was amazingly bleary eyed and, either acting or genuinely, surprised at the commotion! The police were brilliant, and a message came secretly to the nurse involved to go down to the police station and give her side of the story. The police accepted it was a simple prank and let them off with a warning not to do it again. Home Sister never did find out who was to blame, and when I look at that sheer wall I can hardly believe he had the audacity to do it.

Work has not been as good as usual. I'm not overly happy on Hatton (women's medical) and yesterday evening I got very down and even hated it. It is the biggest Nightingale ward I've worked on so far. Actually I prefer these wards, for although they lack privacy for the patients, it is easier to see when they need help. Unusually it has not one but two sisters, who are both ultra efficient, and an elderly spinster staff nurse who makes my life as uncomfortable as possible. I got to the stage where I just wanted a good cry.

I came back to the nurses' home to find the girl next door decidedly downhearted because she's started at Chesterton Hospital (geriatrics) and hates it. I cheered her up a bit and then went round to Angie's room to find her in tears: "Because I'm so fed up, I just don't care about anything anymore". I've noticed that Angie's gentle personality seems to make her more prone to depression than the rest of us. I made her a cup of coffee and listened until she had calmed down. Then I returned to my own room, seriously wondering why we are nurses. Why do we do it? We slave away for little thanks and even less money; we put up with the petty rules and practically become nervous wrecks trying to ensure we don't get told off, but it seems to be inevitable. We get overtired and at times terribly lonely, and yet we all walk around laughing and joking on duty. The patients always say how kind and cheerful the nurses are, but I don't think they realise that their appreciation is the only thing that keeps us going. The strange thing is that, despite all the tears and questioning the purpose of it all, the thought of giving up never occurs to us. Is that what 'vocation' means?

Work today has been much better despite two deaths, both when I was at lunch. I was working with a staff nurse who likes me. She even said, "Did you know we are going to be on nights together? How super." That must be the most un-staff-nurse-ish comment I've ever heard. She works really hard to encourage the juniors and to protect us from the wrath of the sisters.

I've been to the Art's Theatre to see Found in a Handbag, a musical based on Oscar Wilde, and a very odd play called Summer starring Jane Asher. Next week the Ballet Rambert is coming. It is the best thing ever being able to see all these shows for free. The sales are on at the moment with lots of things I'd love to buy, but a medical textbook had to come first. Then I bought some sweet peas and strawberries as a treat.

29th July 1968

I've just spent the afternoon asleep. I've had a run of four early mornings, which always make me feel extra tired, especially as I've worked seven consecutive full shifts on a very busy ward. Important thing is I coped, although I must admit I am counting the days to leaving Hatton. I'm tired of the stupid fuss over silly little things and continuous bickering between the sisters which doesn't make for a good working atmosphere. On the plus side the patients make it all worthwhile. One elderly lady, who has been unconscious for three months since she had a stroke, is now fully awake, and although she is paralysed down one side it is rewarding to watch her progress. She pulled her nasogastric tube out yesterday so we decided to try spoon feeding her and she managed soup and ice cream for lunch. We gave her a haircut, which much improved her appearance, and she sits propped up on pillows, watching everything with such a twinkle in her eyes that I'm sure she is silently laughing at us. Liz is often on the same shifts as me and we enjoy working together. Hatton is easier with a friend beside you, especially one like Liz who sees the funny side of everything. We have one enormous patient who weighs at least twenty stone. I've never seen anyone so overweight before. She comes from Steeple Bumpstead where she still lives with her five brothers and sister, even though they are all in their sixties, because none of them ever married. They all come in together to visit her and are all the same rounded shape, like Tweedledum and Tweedledee in triplicate. She likes Liz and me because between us, and despite the differences in our height, using the Australian lift we can get her on and off the bedpan safely, which is pretty impressive I can tell you. We feel quietly proud that we can help her keep some dignity because she is a gentle person with a simple soul, and her family give us lots of eggs!

The powers that be have hushed up the news on the liver transplant so much that we can't find out the cause of death at all, and I read in the newspapers that another heart transplant patient has died too. Is all this experimenting a good idea or does it just give false hope? It makes you wonder, doesn't it?

Tomorrow is pay day. I'm hoping for a nice fat cheque as I'll have to cycle down on my day off to get it. Thank you again for the unexpected treat of lunch the other day. Gill loved it too and was grateful to be included, a million times better than hospital food!

15th August 1968

I'm on nights again and writing whilst it is quiet, the lull before the storm no doubt. We've been very busy. I was exhausted and slept ten hours the first two days. Whoever said deaths come in threes was right! By a fluke I missed the first two, but then it was my turn and my first dead body was the fourteen-year-old girl. Do you remember, I told you Prof Calne had got permission from the relatives to use her liver for transplant. At five in the morning I heard her crying and went in to see her in the side ward. She calmed down, but whilst I was fetching the bed bath trolley she slipped away. We couldn't believe it because it was so quick, and we'd been anticipating her death for so long that we'd almost ceased to expect it. Anyway, Staff Nurse dashed to the phone to tell the transplant team, whilst the other two of us closed her eyes, straightened her out and tidied her up.

When Staff Nurse returned, she asked, "Is this your first?" and I suddenly realised that it was, and yet it hadn't bothered me at all, though later I felt a bit shaky. I wished I'd stayed with her those last few minutes. Prof Calne couldn't use her liver as he was in the middle of a kidney transplant operation. I was glad because the girl had been so ill, and now looked wonderfully peaceful lying there in her white paper shroud. Then I had to wrap her in the mortuary sheet. I found myself whispering "Goodbye" as in God be with you as I lowered the final top corner over her face. I'd done everything I could for her. Now I know Last Offices is not scary, but a quiet and noble feeling of rounding off the care for a person. There is no doubt in my mind, now I've seen it, that the spirit has gone and only the body is left. There is nothing to be frightened of.

The trouble with the ward being quiet is it becomes very difficult to stay awake.

Continued later:

Famous last words; as I wrote that it all happened. A lady, an emergency admission last night, is in a bed near the desk so we can keep a close eye on her as she is young with a serious heart problem and wired up to various cardiac monitors. The elderly lady in the bed opposite suddenly sat up and complained of chest pain. I went over, and just as I was enquiring if she thought it was indigestion, she keeled over with a heart attack.

I called Staff Nurse, and she said, "Cardiac Arrest, you keep the other patient calm." Before you could blink, the lady was on the floor for CPR and the resuscitation team had arrived with all their gear. They got her going again and back to bed, attached to numerous monitors. The lady I was now looking after was in prime position to watch all this and was understandably upset, with the stress causing her heart to be all over the place. Eventually the resuscitation team moved the elderly lady into a side ward, which I guess means there is not much hope, but she was still hanging on when I came off duty. I found it a bit of a shock that someone can be asking for a cup of tea because they can't sleep, but otherwise seems perfectly OK, and an hour later they are at death's door. On the other hand I was impressed and reassured to see how quickly the doctors arrive to help when we need them.

On the morning of 21st August we arrived on duty to find all the maids in tears and incapable of work. Russia had invaded Czechoslovakia overnight, and most of the maids came from that area. It was impossible for us, born after the war and living in peace, to comprehend the significance of this disaster that had occurred in their already difficult lives. All we could do was offer tea and sympathy and do their work for them.

> *Addenbrooke's Hospital*
> *17th September 1968*

Dear Mrs Walker,

Thank you for your letter giving Eileen permission to become non-resident.

I think the non-residence is satisfactory on the whole, but I would like to draw your attention to these points which I think may have disadvantages. The journeys on and off duty in the early mornings and late evenings are sometimes a little trying, especially in the winter months, and you will appreciate, of course, that we shall have no check on the hours kept at night, although I hope Eileen can be trusted to be sensible in this respect.

We shall continue to give her every care while on duty, and if she should be ill at any time she can be admitted to the Nurse's Sick Bay if necessary. Mrs Kay, Welfare Officer to the non-resident students, will be visiting your daughter from time to time, and if there are any points concerning your daughter's non-residence which you would like us to bear in mind I should be glad if you would let me know.

Overnight male visitors are not allowed, and your consent as well as mine is required if brothers are put up on occasion. I am sure you will appreciate the necessity for this rule.

It is your daughter's responsibility to provide bed linen, etc. for her accommodation. It is forbidden to borrow hospital property. Mrs Kay has authority to make spot checks as necessary.

Yours sincerely,
M.M. Puddicombe
Matron.

ADDENBROOKE'S HOSPITAL
NON-RESIDENT STUDENT NURSES
RULES TO BE OBSERVED

1 No articles to be taken or borrowed from the hospital premises and used in the student's accommodation; if this practice continues it will be necessary for Mrs Kay, the Welfare Officer, to make periodic inspections of the students' accommodation.

2 Rents must be paid promptly on the date specified by the landlord or agent. Gas and electricity bills must be settled, or a forwarding address given to the respective companies before leaving the accommodation.

3 Large and noisy bottle parties cannot be allowed; these disturb neighbours, cause furniture to be broken and subsequently harm the good name of the staff and hospital.

4   Where accommodation includes gardens, these must be kept tidy; beer, wine and milk bottles, plus old cycles, must be disposed of before vacating the premises. All accommodation must be kept clean and left clean at the termination of the tenancy. All broken furniture and missing articles to be replaced. Mrs Kay will advise over this if necessary.

5   Overnight male visitors are not allowed in the student's accommodation.

6   All accommodation must be inspected and approved by Mrs Kay. When a student nurse changes her address she must notify the Assistant Matron immediately.

7   In the event of illness, or any other cause preventing a nurse reporting for duty at the expected time, she must telephone or get a friend to telephone Matron's office immediately. Do not wait to report absence from duty until the time of commencement of the shift.

8   Punctuality. Nurses are expected to report punctually on duty at all times. A nurse who is late on more than two occasions may be asked to become resident again.

Gill found the perfect house. It was a lovely semi-detached property in the village of Trumpington and, although further out of Cambridge, it had the advantage of being equidistant from both the Old and New Sites, and was probably too far for the dreaded Mrs Kay to come checking up on us! Situated on the main road, it was close to shops and, more importantly, there were six pubs within crawling distance. We had a small front garden with lawn, shrubs and a garage for our bikes. The back garden was rectangular with apple trees and roses, a shed and fuel bunkers. The front door opened onto a long thin hallway with a door to the kitchen ahead and the entrance to the lounge on the right opposite the cloakroom and staircase. Behind the lounge was a small dining room with a circular table, ideal for squeezing lots of chairs around for sociable meals. The lounge was pleasantly furnished in a modern style with what turned out to be a very efficient paraffin heater in the fireplace. The kitchen was wonderfully well equipped with a washing machine, a cooker, a fridge, a solid fuel boiler which heated the water, an immersion heater (which we couldn't afford to use) and a drying cabinet (which was invaluable). There was cutlery and crockery; in fact everything we needed except for an electric kettle! Upstairs there were three double bedrooms, a bathroom and a spacious airing cupboard. We looked longingly at the electric storage heaters in the downstairs rooms, but never aspired to using them because the rent would be 13 guineas a month each (plus electricity and fuel) *if* we could find a fifth person. We knew money would be tight, especially the first month when we would be paying for the nurses' home as well because we wouldn't get permission to move out until the end of October. Thank goodness we could eat free meals at the hospital.

As the previous tenants had left the house in a mess we negotiated with the landlady, volunteering to clean it if she would let us off half the first month's rent – anything to save money, and we knew we should have struck a better bargain when she accepted with alacrity! We set to with a will, clearing the cupboards and using the dining room as a general dumping ground. I threw away bags full of rubbish, including the disgusting find of a dirty nappy growing mould at the back of a cupboard. Gill fixed all the electric plugs; she's so practical, but she is also scared of spiders. She chased hundreds of the little blighters with the vacuum cleaner whilst Angie and Liz washed the lounge walls to remove a thick layer of nicotine. The whole house got an enthusiastic spring clean.

Then we tackled the garden. I had never used a motor mower before and the grass was six inches high. The mower kept getting stuck, and then I'd come to a patch I had already mown and the silly thing would zoom off with me in hot pursuit, which was all very well until I came face to face with a rose bush, veered sideways and flew straight through a pile of grass cuttings that Gill had painstakingly raked up, scattering them to the four winds. We laughed and laughed. The sense of freedom was exhilarating; everything was fun and hilariously funny. The house was a huge distraction, but also an incentive to pass our Green Block exam and get our second year belts. We worked hard at the house, but needed to study diligently too because we were financially committed and would not be allowed to move out if we failed.

Letter home:

24th September 1968

We have decided to call our house 'The Nursery', and Gill's boyfriend's father is painting a sign for us. I've sent the landlady the £20 deposit. It will be the four of us and Rita, who you haven't met yet, but she and Angie are good friends. They are having the back bedroom (they chose first and preferred the more peaceful view over the garden), which leaves Gill and me in the largest one at the front (suits us, more room for all our things) and Liz gets the double bed in the smallest room. We have given it all a thorough clean over the weekend and it looks so much better. As soon as possible we are going to take tins of food and have our first supper there, hoorah!

Last week I realised why Fen Causeway is so called. The Granta burst her banks and the whole of the Fen was submerged. Grantchester Meadows was one huge lake and looked very scenic. The far side of the river from the Garden House Hotel was entirely under water and a cow drowned. This morning the river was still overflowing, but the level doesn't appear to be rising any more. Pity, as it would have been entertaining if the ground floor of Owlstonecroft had flooded.

Tomorrow I get my ward report, ho hum! Apparently some of the practical exams aren't until 21st October. It is so silly, why didn't we take them whilst we knew the patients and the ward before we came into block?

First I have to survive Green Block exam. I must go to bed and hope a good night's sleep compensates for not spending enough time revising.

The answer to our rent problem was Rita, an obvious choice as she and Angie were friends and had a lot in common. The two of them were happy to share a room, and the rest of us were pleased to welcome Rita. During the first year our set had split into several sub-sets who moved out to share houses together. Rita was not already part of a defined group, but was friendly with everyone in the set. She was petite, slight and theatrical, with bright blue eyes and masses of long, curly blonde hair. Her moods reflected the weather: spring sunshine brought euphoria with singing, but grey cold days led to silence and an air of sadness. This was understandable when we learnt that her parents divorced when she was two and her mother had brought her up alone. Then her mother died of renal failure when Rita was only eleven, and her childminder became her foster mother, providing a kindly second home for her. In many ways Rita and I were opposites as she lived for the moment whilst I carried my past and planned ahead. Happily Gill, Liz and Angie bridged the extremes and all boded well for a congenial household. Rita, and her guitar, had found a new home at The Nursery.

Second Year

28th September 1968

I hate this new two tier postal system. I never seem to get any letters at all now and keep hoping they are stuck on their way here. I've decided to put a five penny stamp on this time. First class may cost an extra penny, but it is cheaper than phoning; sent second class it would probably take a week to arrive.

We've decided to leave the phone disconnected at the house because, for certain, we won't be able to afford luxuries, especially if one of us fails Intermediate and can't move out. The exam results won't be out until the fifteenth so keep your fingers crossed.

The house is sparkling clean and will feel like home as soon as there is more of our clutter around. Last Saturday we tackled the garden. Our antics with the petrol lawnmower would have made you laugh, but we've tamed the beast. We've done most of the weeding, using discarded rubber gloves from the hospital to keep our hands clean and beautiful for sterile nursing procedures on the wards. You'll notice a huge difference when you next come. Unfortunately my back aches and I've blisters from all the hoeing.

We went round to meet our neighbours, an elderly couple. She kept saying, "I'm sure we can get along together". I suspect she's trying to convince herself that having five noisy nurses next door will be all right.

We've started our new wards. I'm on Bowtell (male, gen-

61

itourinary). It is reputedly the best run ward in the hospital and everything is done 'just so'. The sister is thyrotoxic: always on duty, takes no meal breaks and has eyes and ears like a hawk. I was finding it all a bit bewildering and terrifying until this morning when I suddenly saw the funny side of it all and, as long as I keep my sense of humour, I should survive.

Gill, Liz and I went to Harvest Festival Evensong at Holy Trinity and it reminded me of home. It was a lovely service, but all that food on display made us feel hungry and we'd missed supper. Gill is counting the days until Henry comes up. I'm looking forward to meeting this 'perfect' boyfriend and hope he has some dishy friends!

By the way, the Intermediate exam at the end of Green Block was worryingly easy; in fact, if I fail I had better give up nursing on the spot. My ward report seems to have got lost, but I must tell you about my interview:

Principal Tutor: "Why do you look so disgruntled?"

Me: "Oh dear, does it show? I try to hide it."

Her: "It's good to show our feelings, why?"

Me: "Because I'm bored stiff. The pace of the lectures is so slow it is hard to keep awake"

Her: "OK. If you find it easy, why not get into the subject deeper and study privately for your Diploma in Nursing?"

Me, thinking: "She might like being a spinster sister tutor, but I intend to get married." Mumble something about contact with patients.

Her: "What are you going to do when you finish training?"

Me: "I shall probably staff for a while, but my ambition is primarily to get married and have a family."

Her: "How far has this little plan got? Are you engaged?"

Me: "Good heavens, no, I haven't even found him yet!"

Well she had to laugh at that, but I thought perhaps it was time to stop joking and sound keen again and muttered something about doing midwifery. Still, you should have seen her face, it was a scream.

I came top in the Green Block written exam and we all passed the practical, but, unfortunately, overall Liz failed Intermediate. The other four of us moved to The Nursery, confident that she would knuckle down to more revision and soon pass the resit and come to join us.

Because of a lucky wrong number we discovered the phone would ring with incoming calls and had not been properly disconnected. We proceeded to take advantage of this as boyfriends and family could phone us, but we didn't have to pay any bills. Inevitably it didn't last long, but was a huge bonus meanwhile!

Letter to all at home:

20th October 1968

Living in The Nursery is wonderful; so, so much better than at Owlstonecroft. We love it. Mostly we all get on fine and little disagreements are soon sorted out. We are rarely all together; as you can imagine there is a lot of coming and going on different shifts and notes left in the kitchen. We've got rotas for cleaning and a house kitty for basic shopping and it all seems to be working well. Visitors are always welcome, especially when they come with food parcels.

Gill, Rita and I are thinking of auditioning for the Hospital Revue which will be staged in December. Neither acting nor dancing holds any appeal for Liz and Angie, but they have assured us they will come and laugh at us if we get in.

Bowtell is turning out better than I expected. Sister keeps us all on our toes, but is very fair with praise as well as constructive criticism. The men are good fun and there is lots of joking. I've learnt many new techniques like bladder washouts for the post-op prostatectomies, but I hate the smell of the formaldehyde in the urine bottles; the whole sluice seems to smell of it and it makes my eyes water. I am feeling more confident looking after the drips (intravenous infusions) and am better at adjusting them when they are going through too fast or too slow. We have to count the drip rate per minute, which is why they are called 'drips'. Surprisingly it is not embarrassing doing the dressings on male catheters and tying gauze bows on the end of the penis as most of the men find it funny too. I've learnt to pour Guinness like a proper barmaid. The men are allowed one drink of either stout or Guinness (courtesy of the NHS) at lunchtime to help their waterworks. They all find it very amusing watching naive nurses make a real hash of pouring them and delight in telling us how to do it properly.

Night duty is more relaxed without Sister observing our every move, but when we've been busy with lots of first night post-ops it can be a real scramble to get everything spick and span before she swoops in at the crack of dawn. The patients are wonderfully co-operative and definitely on our side.

4th December 1968

Dear Daddy,

It is a year today since I came home from Sick Bay and I wanted to write especially to you to tell you I really appreciate having a loving home to return to.

You've probably heard already that my school friend Lynne had her baby, Sarah Katherine, on 14th November and has asked me to be Godmother. I feel honoured, but also slightly daunted as it seems a very grown up role.

Last night Gill, Angie and I went to the Advent Carol Service at Great St Mary's Church. There must have been five hundred people, all with candles stuck on squares of cardboard, and more candles in the beautiful flower arrangements. Most people were our age group and the atmosphere was tremendously moving. Never before have I sung so well; the harmony and strength were so great that the organ was completely drowned out in the last verse of 'Oh Come all ye Faithful'.

When we came out of church there were lots of people we knew to say hello to and it was such a happy, friendly gathering.

I can't find appropriate words to express it, but perhaps to say "The light of the Holy Spirit shone in everyone's eyes and peace was in their hearts" is not a bad attempt.

Work has been nerve-racking. The last two days I've been on Ward 2 (heads and neurosurgery). I spent one afternoon specialling a very ill man; that means I looked after him all the time and stayed right by his side. He cardiac arrested and died five minutes after I was relieved, what a narrow escape. This led to two kidney transplants. Today I was asked to escort a seriously ill boy down to X-ray. He needed almost continuous suction and his airway was liable to obstruct if I judged the timing wrong. The porters have never moved a huge traction bed at quite such a speed, with me trying to keep up and look after the patient at the same time. The whole X-ray Department leapt to attention as we flew in, and they couldn't bundle us back out into the corridor fast enough afterwards.

I must go and get ready to 'prance' at the Hospital Revue rehearsal. A bit of light relief!

Letter home:

7th December 1968

I eventually got my increased pay on Wednesday, £36:1s:7d this month, not bad eh?

Gill looked stunning for the Med Soc Ball. I helped her get ready and set her hair quite beautifully; we were both delighted with the result. She's so happy now her Henry is here at Selwyn, another college I am getting to know well. Annie went to the ball too, with Henry's friend Nigel. Previously Gill invited Annie to join a crowd of them celebrating Henry's birthday, a chance I had to turn down because I was on duty that night. Funnily Annie and Nigel seem to have really hit it off so maybe I did her a big favour! They have another friend, Dick, whom I like a lot. He seems pleasantly familiar, a real boy-next-door type. We had hopes of pairing him with Angie, but it didn't work. Apparently Dick has a girlfriend back home. I do wish they could find someone special for me. I am fed up with the lads I've been seeing on and off and have decided to make a clean break with all of them before the end of term and make a fresh start in the New Year.

Gill and Henry were very much a couple. Their year apart had stood the test of time and they were overjoyed to be together again. As soon as he was settled in at Selwyn, Gill took me round to meet him. I came face to face with a tall, slim lad with unruly curly hair and big friendly eyes in a choirboy face. I liked him instantly. His eyes twinkled as they met mine, showing he knew Gill had told me lots about him and he was totally comfortable with that. His voice came as a surprise; how could Gill have forgotten to mention the gentle Welsh lilt that nodded to his ancestry, but combined harmoniously with the Potteries twang? Seeing them together I knew Gill and Henry were meant for one another and I was happy for them.

Soon after that Gill and I met Nigel, who was a medic too and had a room nearby. Nigel was tall and solid, an enthusiastic rugby player with a public school turn of phrase. He gave me all embracing bear hugs of friendship, and he, Henry and Dick teased me constantly in a brotherly way and nicknamed me 'Lanky'. As there was never a romantic spark between any of the lads and me we had a comfortable relationship.

In no time Annie and Nigel became a pair. Annie was one of a foursome from our set, which included Dawn, and they kept their house in Ross Street neater and tidier than anyone else's. Annie was little, dark haired, sociable and kindly. She was, and is, the sort of person whose door is ever open and who is always pleased to see you.

Often all of us would be at the same parties and it was like having an extended family. We set a pattern for the future and we have all stayed friends despite the passing years and geographical divides.

Addenbrooke's Hospital Revue Society presented Puss in Surgical Boots at the ADC Theatre on 18th, 19th, 20th and 21st

December at 8.30pm with a matinee performance on 21st December at 5pm. Tickets 5s.

Rita was Puss (wearing the white wellies that were worn in Old Site Theatres). Gill, Annie and I were in the dancing chorus, the Chirurgical Cuties. From the day of the auditions we loved the whole experience and made the most of the chance to get to know other members of the hospital staff. Rehearsals took up most of our spare time and there were several Revue Parties too. It was exciting to learn we were to perform in a real theatre and thrilling to discover it had proper dressing rooms, with mirrors surrounded by light bulbs. There was a wonderful narrow back staircase that spiralled up to the stage, making us feel like a proper chorus line as a voice over the intercom called "Overture and beginners, please" and we climbed up single file to the wings, trying not to make a clatter with our tap shoes, ready for the opening number.

> We're certainly not complaining,
> Rather the reverse,
> It's terribly spiffing in Cambridge,
> Being a student nurse.
> We're awfully dedicated,
> Especially after ten,
> 'Cos for every girl in term time,
> There's at least three dozen men.
> Since we've come here straight from school,
> In by midnight is the rule,
> But if we're entertaining late,
> We have to rely on the fire escape.
> It's terribly spiffing in Cambridge,
> Being a student nurse,
> We put in long hours,
> But things could be worse.
> Life's fun in Cambridge,
> Life's fun in Cambridge,
> Being – A – Stu – dent – Nurse!

The revue was loosely based on pantomime with a hospital bias to the story line. There were new lyrics to well known song tunes, in jokes and lots of energetic dance routines. Fortunately only a minority wanted to be in the cast, mostly those who had taken part in school drama productions or attended dance classes, leaving the rest of the hospital staff, friends and families to buy tickets. They came to be entertained...and they obviously were. They laughed in all the right places, and at some unexpected mishaps too! The applause was thunderous as they enthusiastically clapped all the dances and shouted for encores after the songs. Five performances whizzed by and all too soon the curtain fell for the last time. It was a dramatic contrast to work on the wards and fantastic fun.

Letter home:

26th December 1968

On Christmas Eve we went to Midnight Mass and then opened all our presents at 2am! Christmas Day passed quickly, and work was much more enjoyable than I expected. Despite it being my first Christmas away from home, the atmosphere was very festive, both amongst the staff and the patients, even here at Chesterton, the geriatric hospital. Lots of bottles of booze were given to the staff, and I decided that if sherry is an acquired taste then if I drink it all the time I should get to like it, especially now my year of abstinence is over. I found I got light-headed quite quickly and have had to pace myself rather more slowly than some of the others. Nothing like a drink to make even boring routine seem hilarious.

One patient is a splendid, autocratic and aristocratic spinster lady who is 103 years old, the oldest person I have ever met. The Bishop came to visit her, and I went in to check she was tidy and she announced, "The Bishop can wait, I need the commode!" I had to get it, help her on, and then go and explain. Fortunately the Bishop thought it was amusing.

Now I am a second year I am sometimes the most senior nurse on the ward. This can be a bit intimidating, especially today when someone died. Actually I was more worried about the junior than myself. It was her first experience of death and she freaked out when we turned the dead lady over to wash her back and the air expelled from the lungs in a deep sigh! When Sister got back from lunch she took over the responsibility of contacting the relatives which let me off the hook. They came in later and I could honestly tell them their mother had passed away peacefully, which was a nice thing to be able to do. At least she didn't die sitting on the commode like one old boy did!

Another time when I was in charge I asked the junior to go round and clean all the false teeth. Later I walked into the sluice to find her scrubbing them all diligently in one big bowl, horrors. I couldn't believe that she had collected them like this and now had no idea which belonged to whom. She was mortified when I pointed out her mistake. Fortunately most of them were plates with only some teeth on, and there were only two full sets for people with very differently shaped mouths; what a stroke of luck. She won't ever do that again and thanks her lucky stars she avoided the wrath of Sister or Staff Nurse. I was too worried at the time to see the funny side of this, but when I told the others back at The Nursery we laughed and laughed.

20th January 1969

A belated Happy New Year! I've been so busy there hasn't been a moment to put pen to paper, but as you'll be wondering what I've been up to, here is the latest social news.

Last Friday I went to a party at Selwyn, given by Henry, Nigel, Dick and their friends, which was so-so. It should have been fun, but Nigel and Henry kept pulling my leg, and every time they passed me they whispered, "Have you found him yet?" Usually I enjoy their teasing, but that night I wished I had never said I was going to find 'the one' this term. Then everyone paired off about eleven o'clock, and rather than look like a wallflower I came home as I had to get up early.

The next night I went to the Eightsome's housewarming party. (Eight girls in our set moved into a large house together.) I wore that new black linen shift dress with the white lace collar which I finished making in the nick of time. It was a super evening and I met a nice chap called Peter who is a third year mathematician at Churchill and has got a car. I could hardly believe it, a car! It was a big plus point in his favour, though his chat up line "I suppose you are another nurse" was not exactly inspired. He offered me a lift home, but I needed to cycle back as I was on duty first thing the next morning and needed the bike in the right place.

I've agreed to see him again.

The party was in full swing when a lad, Peter, appeared by my side and attempted to start a conversation. At the time my attention was fixed on the door and some new arrivals: Robert, whom I had dumped unceremoniously at the end of the previous term, with a new girlfriend on his arm. I felt exposed and determined that he should not notice I was on my own. What else could a girl do? I grabbed the lifeline this poor lad had unwittingly extended, chatting back in an animated manner. Whilst laughing and hanging on to his arm as if we had the closest of relationships, I steered the two of us under Robert's nose and into the other room where there was dancing to lively music. Peter couldn't believe his luck; never had a chat up line worked so well!

Just as I thought I was safe and could make my excuses and disappear, someone turned the lights off and changed the record to create a romantic mood. Peter's arms encircled me and I was trapped. What had I done? I had led this lad on and I hadn't even looked at him properly. I felt the rough tweed of his sport's jacket against my bare arms, and although he was shorter than me we fitted together surprisingly neatly like two pieces of a jigsaw. We swayed to and fro, step together, step together, and somehow my cheek came to rest against his clean shaven one. I took a hesitant breath: no nicotine, thank goodness. He smelt of soap with a hint of aftershave: clean, fresh and reassuring. Perhaps this was going to be OK.

The records changed, but we stayed comfortably together. After a while he tried to kiss me and I decided to let him, curiosity overriding caution. That first kiss was gentle, tentative and enquiring. Spontaneously my lips responded with a silent 'try that again…and again…and again'! I suppose there must have been some conversation for me to have established and remembered his name, year and college. Certainly the exchange about the car and where I lived came only at the very end of the evening when I reluctantly tore myself away. I knew embarrassingly little about Peter, except his touch and taste which felt quite extraordinarily addictive. Of course I agreed to see him again!

26th January 1969

I'm writing again because I've got so much to say a telephone call would be too expensive and it's the end of the month. I've been having an absolutely fantastic time and am feeling fit and healthy. Yesterday the weather was spring-like and I was in such a good mood that I sped to Chesterton in twenty minutes and didn't even get puffed going up Castle Hill. I'm on the Outpatient Clinic for a week, which is more like office hours and makes a civilised change.

On Wednesday we went to the Post-Hospital-Revue party to listen to the tape recording and get our photos. As usual the gigantic bowl of punch had a powerful effect and some of the doctors had to be held at arms' length. One proceeded to tell the whole room that I was such a sensible girl, which was embarrassing. Thursday I went shopping and got some stunning evening shoes with sparkling silver daisies across the straps, which are gorgeous.

Friday was Matron's Ball. I was escorted by another of Henry's friends who has a long-term girlfriend at home, but is good company and was happy to even the numbers up. As before, we started getting ready early in the afternoon.

I washed and set my hair, did my nails, then took ages over my make-up. I brushed my hair out and put it up using that stone brooch you gave me to cover the rubber band. I just managed to be ready by eight o'clock. Fourteen of us met at our house and then took taxis to the Guildhall where the Head Porter from the Old Site acted as commissionaire. The boys, all looking super-smart in their dinner jackets, got us drinks and we sat at a table near the door of the ballroom to watch other people arriving whilst giving a running commentary on what they were wearing.

Later we walked across to the Corn Exchange in search of food. A marquee had been erected inside the building which looked splendid and transformed it into a truly magical place, but it was stiflingly hot, especially with a jazz band, lots of bouncy dancing and stamping of feet. There was a huge cold finger buffet, included in the ticket price, and I ate at least twenty-five lots of delicious asparagus in brown bread. We had proper coffee too. The atmosphere was great; we knew so many more people than last year and I got lots of compliments. I danced on air. The band in the ballroom was excellent and it finished all too soon (at one o'clock) with the usual mounting climax of 'Hokey-Cokey', 'Knees up Mother Brown', the 'Conga' and 'Auld Lang Syne'. Then we came back to the house and opened some fizz which rounded off a nearly perfect evening. I just wished I had been partnered by someone I loved and I felt a bit envious of some of the others. Balls are made for romance.

The next night Peter came to take me out to dinner and explained he'd had to apply for permission to keep his car at the college. He only swung it because he is secretary of the Hockey Club and can drive members to matches. He was wearing an interesting tie that he says proves he has completed the Cambridge Boundary Run; it is quite a status symbol to have run over 25 miles. Few students attempt it, and even less complete the course!

He took me to The Plough at Fen Ditton. Wow, this is

the life! I had a sweet martini, then melon, roast chicken and asparagus served with tomato and peas, followed by my favourite apple pie and cream, coffee and After Eight mints. We shared half a bottle of Entre Deux Mers, and as he was driving I had most of it. I was well and truly wined and dined, and it cost him £4 too. For the first time I wondered if someone was actually going to try and seduce me. When he stopped the car in a dark lay-by I had to laugh. Anyway, you'll be pleased to know he didn't – didn't even try.

He's very nice. He's taking me out for a drink tonight.

Our first date provided the opportunity for me to discover more about Peter. There was plenty of time to talk and for me to look at him properly. I liked what I saw. Always before I had been attracted to, and chosen to go out with, stereotypical tall, dark, handsome, extrovert lads. This was completely different; fate had thrown us together. Peter was about three inches shorter than me, unbelievably quiet and introverted. He was master of the pregnant pause. When I asked him a question there would be a disconcertingly long silence whilst I waited impatiently for the answer. This didn't appear to be deliberate, nor a speech impediment, just a defining characteristic that took a bit of getting used to. Fortunately, in getting to know Angie, I had learnt that silence is not necessarily threatening, but can be both calming and companionable.

I found Peter intriguing and our conversations stimulating. When we talked he looked me directly in the eye, was content to let me chatter on and was an attentive audience. When he laughed it was uproariously, an explosion from uncharted depths within him. Unusually for a boy he did not expect me to listen adoringly whilst he talked endlessly about sport or cars, and he treated me as if I was equally intelligent even though I was not at the university.

On 29th January Peter introduced me to his room in Churchill College. I admired the stark modern architecture of this new college and thought it an impressive memorial to a great man. It was the first college in Cambridge to be focused on science, engineering and technology rather than humanities and to admit a larger proportion of its undergraduates, such as Peter, from state schools. Built as an all male college, officially opened by the Duke of Edinburgh in 1964, it later became the first Cambridge College to decide to admit women (as had been Churchill's wish) in 1972. It had the largest dining hall of all the Cambridge colleges and was the first college to have central heating in the students' rooms, which was much appreciated by us, though I missed being able to toast crumpets on a gas fire! Peter explained there had been a huge disagreement over whether there should be a Chapel. It was built eventually, but is sited away from the main buildings on the far side of the playing fields.

Written from my parents' house:

4th February 1969

Dear Peter,

Thank you for your letter which I received this morning when Mother woke me at eleven o'clock. Oh, what a life of luxury, being spoilt at home.

I'm afraid I won't be able to see you next Saturday. My cousin has just married an Indian and she is bringing him to meet us. Normally I'd simply say, "Terribly sorry, got to be back at work", but under the circumstances, when it might be interpreted as colour prejudice, I can't. The whole situation is a bit touchy so I've got to put the family first, though I'd rather be with you.

Saturday night we visited the only local cinema to see Thoroughly Modern Millie which I loved, especially the tap dancing in the lift.

Shortly after I posted this letter there was a panic phone call from Cambridge. Liz was the only one at the house, the rest of us being on holiday and away. She had arrived back one morning after night duty to discover the fire brigade putting down sawdust to soak up the water which had been pouring out under the front door. Apparently the postman had spotted it and called them. My parents drove me to Cambridge immediately to assess the damage and to help us negotiate with the landlady.

We waited anxiously for the emergency plumber's verdict that 'The pipe carrying the mains water supply to the storage tank in the attic pulled away from the joint at the ballcock. It is likely that the extreme temperatures had caused this to happen.' It was good news that it wasn't our fault, but the house was drenched and uninhabitable. The others moved to stay with friends or back into the nurses' home, and it was agreed I would stay with the next-door neighbours to be nearby and let workmen in as necessary. Although I felt slightly awkward, the neighbours were very hospitable, spoiling me with hot meals when I got home and the luxury of an electric blanket, which meant I slept in seventh heaven. They, like many people in those days, thought that nurses ought to be cherished. They could not have been kinder.

Obviously the hospital had to be informed of the change in circumstances. Fortunately Matron was sympathetic and approved our temporary accommodation.

Letter home:

1st March 1969

On Friday night I am going to a pyjama party with Peter in the cricket pavilion at the college. I decided to invest in a gorgeous new nightie. It's a very pretty blue colour with lots of pleated chiffon layers and satin ribbons like a Charleston dress. It was great to have a good excuse to buy it as I've admired it in the shop window for ages. Now I need a lovely pair of fluffy mules and I shall feel a million dollars.

We are all back in the house and managing amidst the chaos; it is very difficult to tip-toe quietly on bare boards. The insurance assessor has been, and painters will start redecorating in April when the plaster has dried out. The landlady was supposed to come last night, but didn't turn up. However everything seems to be under control and she has agreed we shall pay half rent until it is all straight again.

My social life is full as I've been seeing a lot of Peter. We've eaten at the Turk's Head, the Hong Kong Garden and the Ancient Shepherds at Fen Ditton, which is my favourite so far. We went to the Arts to see an opera called The Kiss, he's taken me to dine in hall at Churchill and he came to Great St Mary's Church with us. I think our best evening was last Thursday when there was a meeting of the Socratic Society at Churchill, of which Peter is chairman. It's a posh name for an excuse to have a good dinner and then listen to an interesting, well known speaker! More importantly, it felt like my formal introduction to the college as his girlfriend, so I was on my best and most charming behaviour. I had to race home from work and get changed super fast.

In the Buttery we met John Snagge (BBC commentator – Boat Race) who was the guest speaker and the Canon (College Chaplain and coach to the Boat Club) who said, "Who's the bird?", then added, "Any girl with Peter must be good." He bought me a sherry. John Snagge chatted away, telling me amusing stories of his meetings with Prince Philip, Churchill and others. Then we all moved into hall to dine on the centre table and had a rather better meal than everyone else. (Special menu, wine, flowers – the table looked splendid.) Apart from the top table, we entered hall last and it was up to Peter to usher John Snagge in, but, being gentlemen, they insisted I went first. Talk about a grand entrance! It's a good thing I'd had a couple of drinks else I'd never have had the confidence to carry it off. I was the only young female in the room and felt a bit self-conscious wearing a short mini-dress with what felt like hundreds of pairs of male eyes admiring my legs.

During dinner the chap on my other side was flirting with me. He was grey-haired and distinguished looking and turned out to be a Don. He made a point of looking after me for the rest of the evening, as did Peter's three friends; in fact I was in my element. Peter said he had never seen me so lively and vivacious before. I reminded him that he'd never seen me after two glasses of sherry, and two more of wine, surrounded by admiring males! Apparently I was the talk of the college the next day, which pleased Peter. I love the way he is happy for me to be the centre of attention. He may be quiet, but his eyes speak volumes and it is all very flattering. Unfortunately I shall miss the next meeting because I'm on night duty, but Peter's promised to take me again next term.

Back to work now. Life on Private Wards is so slow it is boring me stiff, but the presents from grateful patients are better and I got a pair of one-size tights last week. On the upside, my social life is fantastic. I think you may be surprised when you meet Peter as he is very different from all the other boys I've been out with. He is shy and very conservative in his dress (I can work on that later). He doesn't say much, and says I twitter enough for both of us!

2am, 11th March 1969

Dearest Peter,

Apart from coming to consciousness twice just long enough to realise it was still light, both Gill and I slept through until the alarm went off at 7.45pm. We must have been tired, and it is easier to settle to sleep when two of us are doing it. I feel much better for it.

This is the last lot of nights I'll have to do until August, which in some ways is a pity as I like being up when most people are asleep. I enjoy having time to get all my letter writing done and make progress on the knitting. I prefer the friendlier atmosphere and the feeling that we are trusted rather than that someone is checking up on what we are doing all the time. Also we've discovered that it is easy to make private phone calls from the office as it is possible to get an outside line by simply dialling the right number first. That's the biggest advantage of being on Private Wards: I can phone home for free!

Dawn is visiting me during her break and, whilst enjoying some of the patients' cheese and biscuits (another plus point),

77

we have been having a spook session because she hadn't heard the story of the resident ghost (and I thought she knew everything about the hospital!). The ghost hasn't been seen for ages, but is supposed to be a lady in a grey dress.

Yesterday one of the patients gave me an exotic potted plant with scarlet flowers; she had so many they wouldn't all fit on the floor of her taxi. It will add a splash of colour to my display on the kitchen windowsill.

Liz has had another letter from my big brother. It won't do. I've only ever had three from him in the entire eighteen months I've been in Cambridge, and she's had more than that already. Gill and Henry are madly happy, and Angie is once again 'in love' with her boyfriend back home.

Paul, my big brother, lived in Hereford, and he had decided on the spur of the moment to come and visit me the weekend of the Eightsome's party. This was awkward because I had full shifts both days that weekend and couldn't be with him. Coincidentally it was the weekend Liz was moving out to join the rest of us at The Nursery and none of her family could come with a car to help transfer her belongings. I sent Paul to the rescue, thinking it would give him something to do whilst I was working; certainly it never occurred to me that there would be an instant attraction between him and Liz.

They came to the Eightsome's party together, spent the whole of the next day enjoying each other's company and I hardly saw Paul at all! He became a regular weekend visitor from then on. I was apprehensive about this unexpected relationship. On the one hand I was pleased to see my big brother more often as we had always been close, but on the other his track record with girls was not good and I worried my friend would get hurt. I was also a tiny bit jealous that he was quite obviously more interested in being with Liz than me. Fortunately I was seeing a lot of Peter and there was little room in my mind for anyone other than him. I found him utterly and overwhelmingly attractive.

Letter home:

12th March 1969

Night duty is very quiet with only four patients per nurse. One of them is terminally ill and needs a lot of attention as she is vastly swollen with fluid retention. Because it is difficult moving her she only asks for a bedpan when she is absolutely bursting and she passes huge quantities of urine. One time there was so much the bedpan overflowed; you wouldn't believe a bladder could hold that much! We had to change the whole bed, which was horribly embarrassing and uncomfortable for her. I felt sad as she is a lovely person and tries to be no trouble. Her skin is so hard we have to inject painkillers into her abdomen, but she never complains and always says thank you. Her dignity is inspirational.

Night Sister has cottoned on that we are having a cushy time and is sending me to relieve on ENT (ears, nose and throat) for the meal break.

Gill's on night duty at exactly the same time, which is rather nice because life doesn't seem quite so back to front and upside down. Griffith (men's medical) where she is and Private Ward are joined through the sluice so we see quite a lot of each other during the night, even if only to call out hello. We are a bit fed up to be on nights for the last week of term and are both missing our men.

The pyjama party I went to with Peter was great fun, and on a bottle of wine between the two of us that was hardly surprising. I was very good and cycled home despite the temptation to sleep in college. It would never do for us to get caught and have Peter sent down in disgrace when he is so close to finals. Other girls risk it, but I won't. It is more possible at Churchill than other colleges because it is still being built and you can sign out and say goodnight to the porters and then slip in round the back, whereas in the older colleges you'd have to climb walls – unless someone has an illicit key to a side gate, like the one Father used to have at Trinity!

On Sunday Peter took me to The Pagoda to cheer me up before nights. We've been to all the Chinese restaurants in Cambridge and The Pagoda does the best food, though the décor isn't as impressive as in some of the others.

On 16th March Peter drove me home for Mothering Sunday lunch and met my family. That evening we dined in hall at Churchill, and at bedtime I wrote in my diary, 'I know this is a significant day and the start of something important'.

The next day Peter plucked up the courage to tell me he was Jewish. I looked at him afresh and it was obvious; how come I hadn't noticed his wavy hair, his strong jaw line and his typically Jewish nose before? My love was blind. We were in his car, stopped at a red traffic light. I think he fully expected me to run a mile, but, being a nurse, I didn't. In truth it never crossed my mind for I had already decided he was the one for me, and because he looked so nervous and positively scared, this seemed a good moment to tell him so.

19th March 1969

Dearest Peter,

Apparently Paul and Liz are serious too. Liz told me. Angie reckons we should have 'Time will tell' engraved as the motto of The Nursery. She can be a real pessimist. The more I think about you and me the more certain I become.

I bought some gorgeous jade green material and a new pattern to make a dress for the Christening of my Goddaughter. However I'm not sure that a mini-dress and the role of Godmother aren't a little contradictory. What do you think?

Thanks a million for such a lovely long letter. You are never far from my thoughts and I'm longing to see you again. Sending back your thousand kisses, returned with interest!

On 28th March Peter and I attended the Opening Dinner of the Churchill International Student Conference where the guest of honour was HRH The Duke of Edinburgh.

A college friend of Peter's was one of the organisers and he gave us tickets to the dinner in exchange for my assurance that I'd tell lots of nurses about the party afterwards. The table settings were magnificent with the college silver sparkling in the lights, the flowers and fruit adding colour to the pristine white tablecloths and the menus and place cards all bearing the college coat of arms. It was the closest I had been to royalty since the Queen had come to open the new Brentwood Council Offices when I was in my primary school uniform, waving a flag as her car glided by. This time I wore a scarlet mini-dress, was in the very same room as Prince Philip, ate the many courses of delicious food, enjoyed the wines, listened to the speeches and felt privileged to be a small part of such a prestigious occasion.

At this stage of our training, for the next three months we had to choose between experience in the psychiatric hospital at Fulbourn or the chest and heart speciality at Papworth. Gill, Liz and I chose Fulbourn. Angie and Rita went to Papworth where they had to live in.

Gill had invested in a moped; unlike the rest of us she already had a driving licence, and usually she would ride slowly alongside me, keeping pace with my bicycle. It wasn't long before it occurred to me to put my hand on her shoulder so that Gill could speed up and tow me along. It worked brilliantly and we could go twice as fast. We hoped we would be on the same shifts at Fulbourn and would be able to fly there and back.

31st March 1969

Dearest Peter,

I'm so glad to hear about your job offer, it is the most wonderful news and I'm delighted for you.

It looks as if it won't only be me helping you keep your sanity with finals next term; it's a certainty that without you I would lose mine. I feel as if I was admitted to the psychiatric hospital at Fulbourn today.

Last night I couldn't sleep. I tossed and turned, wondering

what on earth I had committed myself for, and by the time I got up this morning I was practically a gibbering idiot. (Liz and Gill weren't much better.) Even so we made it out to Fulbourn in good time, about twenty minutes' cycling with a rest when Liz's chain came off and she had to fix it. Apparently we do not go into study block for the first three days as we expected, but are to be thrown mercilessly onto the wards. Help! The sister doing the introductory talk produced these huge, heavy keys on an equally large key ring and explained they are our pass keys to get through locked ward doors. Now I was seriously frightened. She assured us doors are very rarely locked; needless to say the first one we attempted to open was!

Then things started to brighten up a bit. Gill and I are working together on the same ward and the same shifts nearly all the time we are here, certainly for the first six weeks. This was brilliant news. We are on 'chronic sick' to start with and can help to keep each other's spirits up. Actually the chronic care is probably the most pitiful and, for me, the more difficult thing to handle. I'm glad we'll have the acute wards to look forward to. The three days' study will come mid-April and I shall be able to see you more then.

There is a rumour that the practical exam in state finals has been abolished. Thank God, that would be such a relief as I get stupidly nervous about practicals and worry I'll make a mess of it. I was starting to feel a bit anti-nursing and even considered chucking it all in, but I know that is silly and often happens in the second year. Now I'm determined to continue, and Fulbourn is apparently very good about off duty requests so going to the Christening shouldn't be a problem. I'm sure I can cope here.

The next morning the alarm went off and neither Gill nor I moved, although we were both awake. Gill whispered, "We must be out of our tiny minds" and I agreed silently. We were both shell-shocked after our first day and petrified by the thought of what might happen next. Somehow we made it back to Fulbourn…and quite quickly we got used to this strange environment.

After the bustle of general nursing this was a huge contrast as we learnt to move slowly and have endless patience. The occupational therapy session lasted most of every weekday morning, and we had to encourage the patients to pack plastic Rawlplugs into cardboard boxes. Some of them couldn't even manage that. Mostly they were institutionalised and robotic as they followed a set routine, the same every day, but the superficial calm could suddenly erupt into violence and we needed to be quick witted and always alert to danger.

One patient was severely brain damaged as a result of a heroin overdose and he was often the flash point. He always seemed to pick on me and several times I was attacked, scratched and bruised. Another lad was there because his ventilator had become disconnected when he was seriously ill as a little boy and the lack of oxygen had caused brain damage and affected his development. He was a teenager now, big and strong, but with the mental age of a seven-year-old. He had eventually learnt to walk normally, but sounded like a Dalek from the Dr Who programmes when he spoke.

Many of the patients were simple souls who had been abandoned in hospital because their family didn't want, or couldn't manage, to care for them and this was the solution. I don't recall any of the patients ever having a visitor in the six weeks we worked there. They were totally dependent and would not be able to cope in the real world because this sheltered lifestyle was all they had ever known. As we spent more time with them they ceased to seem frighteningly abnormal and became eccentric individuals with quirky characteristics. We could never relax completely, but we ceased being quite so tense and this new world became surprisingly normal.

Liz was working on a different chronic sick ward and was very touchy. The work depressed her and she found it very hard emotionally. She took to smoking which she found helped and was easy to do as most of the staff, and patients, smoked too. We all started swearing in a most un-ladylike fashion, a habit we had to learn to suppress outside the hospital environment.

Our biggest problem was getting up in the dark before six o'clock for ten mornings running and finding ourselves exhausted mentally, but not physically despite the long bike rides. Meanwhile the builders were creating chaos at The Nursery re-plastering the lounge ceiling. They were alarmed to hear the three of us were working at Fulbourn, but calmed down when we made them numerous cups of tea. They did try hard not to inconvenience us any more than was inevitable, and told the landlady the electric storage heaters had to be on to dry the plaster out, which was wonderful as the weather was still very cold.

Easter Day, 8th April 1969

Darling Peter,

Funny thing Liz said the other day: "I hate the expression 'darling' except when you and Peter use it, then it sounds natural." Sums up my feelings exactly, Darling, it is right for you and no one else. Guess it's because I love you!

If you phone me when I'm at my parents' house you'll have to go through the operator as Brentwood is still a manual exchange. At least my parents have their own telephone: they used to share a party line with next door, which was awkward.

My lovely big Easter Egg is as yet uneaten, but the contents are. I opened it this morning to find it empty except for a card, 'The Phantom Chocolate Nicker strikes again, ha, ha!' Unsurprisingly, it was in my big brother's handwriting. I had to laugh. I hadn't realised the egg had been tampered with, although all the others knew about it. Amazingly he had given the chocolates to Liz for safekeeping, so I got them anyway. They didn't last long with all of us tucking in.

A storm is gathering over the possibility of student nurses having to pay for their meals. If that happens we will be worse off than before the pay award. I hope enough voices are raised in protest to stop it as we can't work this hard on empty stomachs.

The Nursery is every bit as chaotic as we anticipated. All the lounge furniture is squashed in the dining room and it's like living in an overcrowded mouse hole. Liz is off sick with a throat infection; I hope she doesn't give it to me. Rita is in a cheerful phase and Gill and I can't wait for next Monday and seeing our men.

Need I say it? I'm longing to hear your voice again. I guess my ears should be burning, but, joking apart, I'm glad you told your father about us and got a favourable reaction. I look forward to meeting him, and your mother, though I appreciate her reaction may not be as positive. I must finish and catch the last post. I shall be telling all my friends at home about this truly wonderful person I've met and fallen deeply in love with. I'm completely happy knowing you love me too and I feel as if some unseen magnet pulled us together and my life has changed for ever.

I remember a special evening of the Socratic Society on 4th May. Lee Kwan Yew, Prime Minister of Singapore, was the guest speaker and we had dinner with him and his wife, a formidable woman. It was during that evening Peter and I learnt more about the Canon – Noel Duckworth, Churchill College Chaplain. This short man with a magnetic personality had been an army chaplain. During the evacuation of Singapore he had refused to leave on the last boat, choosing to stay with the wounded and facing certain death. By a quirk of fate, as he ran at the advancing Japanese troops, swearing as only he could, trying to protect his men, he was recognised by a Japanese officer as the cox of the British rowing eight at the Berlin Olympics, the officer having been in the first Japanese boat ever to enter an Olympics. Consequently the men were spared, and although many died later working on the Burma Railway, it is also undeniable that over the years in captivity this unusual Padre won the admiration and gratitude, and helped save the lives, of thousands of soldiers from many parts of the world.

The summer term flew by with Peter working hard for finals, often with me ensconced on his wide window seat, either reading or knitting, waiting patiently for him to finish his sums. We spent a lot of time together in Churchill and I grew fond of the college lifestyle, the buildings, the Hepworth sculpture and especially the chapel. There were more Socratic Society meetings, lots of parties and we dined in hall regularly.

Sarah Katherine was Baptised on 1st June 1969. Somehow, despite the upheaval at The Nursery, my new dress was finished and a cheap but stylish white lace wide floppy brimmed hat bought to complete the outfit for my Goddaughter's Christening. Peter was by my side and it was wonderful to see my school friend with her husband and baby. I wondered how many years it would be before I had a baby of my own to hold.

Letter home:

11th June 1969

Last weekend we went to stay with Peter's parents in their flat over their newsagent's shop. I found his father very easy to chat with and he enjoyed gently teasing us. The first thing I noticed about his mother was that she has a skin condition with very white patches between brown areas, something Peter had not mentioned. She was dressed all in beige (Peter says she rarely wears any colour) and her shoes were too big so she shuffled along (I expect she's got bunions). The flat was colourless too with streamlined Ercol furniture and not a single photograph, ornament or knick-knack in sight. Every surface was clear, very different to what I'm used to. The meal was a bit of a nightmare for me as she piled food on my plate with typical Jewish hospitality, but then asked me a string of questions making it difficult to get a mouthful in between answering. I know Peter eats much quicker than we do and I discovered both his parents eat extremely fast too, so they had all finished when I had hardly started.

His father is going to take us out to dinner on degree day and hopefully that will be easier. Peter has explained that his father's family have lived in England for a long time, but his mother came here to escape the Nazi tyranny in Vienna. She was very lucky to get out of Austria alive, and I assume that whole experience has scarred her for life. The subject is forbidden territory so I guess we'll never know for sure when her mental health problems started. I think I made a good impression, but she is so polite it is difficult to know what she is really thinking.

Having met his parents and seen the flat, I am starting to understand Peter better. As an only child (who kept his head down and worked hard) he has never experienced sibling rivalry, the casual borrowing of personal belongings, back chat and in jokes. I have opened up a whole new world to him. It is hardly surprising it is taking him time to get used to it, and for my Cambridge friends to feel comfortable with him. He doesn't mind being with us all (except when we talk about the hospital as he is a bit squeamish), but he hasn't worked out how to join in yet. I know already that he likes having me all to himself best of all.

I've just woken up after thirteen hours of blissful sleep. What makes you think it was the Churchill May Ball on Monday night? It was called 'Elysium' and was absolutely fantastic. We had such a marvellous time. I may get into the glossies as we had our photo taken by The Tatler! I'll tell you all about it when I see you.

The weather is glorious. I'm roasting, feel drowsy and could easily go back to sleep.

Cambridge May Balls are actually held in June after the exams have finished. They take months of planning, and tickets are expensive as each college aims to create a very special night. At that time most of the colleges headlined a famous pop group as their main attraction. Churchill was a new college without the same financial resources or contacts, and with a stroke of genius the ball committee decided to do something both completely different and unique. They created a fairground complete with sideshows and, best of all, dodgems.

I had spent weeks working on a new evening dress. I didn't have the dressmaking skills to tackle boning, nor enough money to buy a new pattern as well as material. I decided to use the top of the pattern I'd used for the dress I wore to the Christening and added a simple long gathered skirt with a layered net petticoat. I made it in pale blue flocked nylon with a darker blue velvet ribbon for a belt, and I knitted a triangular shawl in white slubbed cotton to go with it. My beautiful silver evening shoes made another appearance and I borrowed an evening bag. Peter hired a dinner jacket with a bow tie and cummerbund. To complete the outfits he bought white carnations for both of us, which were a perfect and thoughtful touch.

We met Steve (he and Peter shared a room in their second year) and his girlfriend Ros (who is one of The Eightsome, Steve and Ros were indirectly responsible for us meeting at that party) and went to The Plough, Fen Ditton for dinner. We started with sherry and then drank a rosé wine with our main course, which was steak with fried eggs, tomatoes, mushrooms, peas, chips and new potatoes. We lingered over coffee and returned to Churchill about 11:30pm to find the ball in full swing. Exchanging our entry ticket, we received vouchers for two glasses of champagne and one glass of Riesling each, and a bottle of specially labelled Rosé d'Anjou between us. We sipped the Riesling whilst we wandered around admiring the transformation to the college that had taken place during the previous few days.

There were several marquees lit by fairy lights with various bands playing at different times, and we joined in the dancing as the mood took us. Later, fortified by a glass of champagne, we visited the fairground and had lots of fun on the dodgems. We chased friends, Fellows and the Master, bashing them about as much as possible. There is no doubt being in dodgem cars or on the carousel in evening dress made it all the more magical. There were no charges so we took turns on the coconut shies and the hoopla stall. We didn't win anything, but the fun really was in the taking part and sharing the excitement with friends.

Eventually we felt hungry again and headed up the staircase to hall where our eyes fell on the most spectacular buffet I have ever seen. On a stand in the centre was the crowning glory of a stuffed peacock with his tail fanned out making an impressive backdrop to huge platters of succulent sliced turkey, ham and rare beef with enormous cut glass bowls full of a variety of salads. On another table there were artistically decorated gateaux: strawberry, chocolate, raspberry, and a delicious looking fresh fruit salad. As if that wasn't enough, a further table groaned under the weight of cheeses, fruit and tempting open boxes of chocolates. Despite the fact that lots of people had been before us, it all looked immaculate and the waiters were dashing about clearing empty plates and replenishing supplies. It reminded me of an illustration for a feast in a fairy story, and click: the camera of my mind took a photo to capture the moment for ever. After eating, we both felt quite sleepy and noticed it was nearly five o'clock; the night was passing all too quickly.

Determined to enjoy every minute we followed the sound of drums to a small marquee that housed a steel band amongst potted ferns. The music was invigorating and we felt compelled to dance the rest of the night away until we staggered into breakfast and picked up our last glass of champagne. We were drunk on alcohol, atmosphere, tiredness and love. Arms entwined and very close, we strolled back towards Peter's room. As we drained the last drop of champagne, I'm ashamed to admit we smashed the glasses against a wall quite deliberately, disappeared through the door and up the stairs to bed. No one else could possibly have had a more marvellous time; we were blissfully happy.

We awoke much later. Peter changed and took me back to The Nursery still in my evening dress, but carrying my shoes because those beautiful silver daisies had become horribly uncomfortable and I had blisters from all the dancing! We never did drink the bottle of Rosé d'Anjou. Rita and Liz polished it off, but I was delighted to have the bottle as a souvenir and made it into a lamp.

Cambridge Tripos results were announced in the *Daily Telegraph* and *The Times* on Friday 20th June. Peter became a Wrangler with a first class Honours Degree in Mathematics.

Envelope addressed with BA (Cantab)
23rd June 1969

Ooh! Ah! Isn't that impressive! I couldn't resist being the first to have the privilege of addressing a letter to you like this. I'm so proud of you, my clever darling.

All my love, always and forever.

Eileen, xx.

I felt very proud of Peter on Degree Day and honoured to be by his side. It was a chilly day, but the biggest cloud was his mother's paranoid behaviour. I knew of her history of mental illness, but now I was seeing it for real. She was convinced we were standing in the wrong place. She thought people were looking at us, talking about us and planning to do us harm. His father's way of coping seemed to be to ignore her, leaving me to talk to her as Peter was not with us until after the ceremony. My training at Fulbourn proved very helpful.

In the evening we were all more relaxed and enjoyed dinner at The Ancient Shepherds in Fen Ditton.

28th June 1969

Darling Peter,

Gill arrived back today but is still poorly, and Liz went off home with her cold. Angie is back and it is great having her sense of humour around again. Rita is her usual self, and Pee-nuts, the kitten she acquired without asking the rest of us, is as much of a nuisance as ever. The name says it all.

I know you don't like me talking about work all the time,

but I thought you'd like to hear this. The tutor handed my case study on the schizophrenic student straight to the consultant psychiatrist who demanded to see me. I was puzzled – why? It turned out all he wanted to say was how excellent he thought my work was and congratulate me. He sees me as a budding psychiatric nurse because he was completely floored to discover a mere general nurse had written it. I am very sad to be leaving Fulbourn today because I have really enjoyed my time working here, especially on the acute wards, though I admit I did find the ECT (electro-convulsive therapy) treatments a bit unnerving to start with. If I wasn't with you I might have seriously considered going on to do some psychiatric training; the workings of the human mind are completely fascinating and these three months have been the most intellectually stimulating so far. I shall miss the men in white coats. Everyone has been very decent and has said super things about us all. They all claim they are sad to see me go...only because they'll have to work harder and won't have my help with the crosswords!

I'm sure there is no need for me to say that I feel the same as you about us being apart for so long, and I'm sure it will feel like ages, but you have the chance of a wonderful holiday touring Europe, albeit three men in a tent. I think you deserve it after all your hard work before finals, and that is more important than me missing you. Keep healthy and happy until I see you again and just remember you take my love, hugs and kisses with you.

Bon voyage.

Airmail letter:

2nd July 1969

Darling Peter,

I know it will be nearly three weeks before you get this, but there is so much to say I thought I'd better start now. I keep thinking I must remember to tell you this, or that, and then by the time I come to write things down I can't recall half of it. Perhaps that is just as well as I know you get bored with hospital gossip.

I think my sister enjoyed her stay here. Mother came down to pick her up and brought us a huge bunch of roses to say thank you. It was a bit 'coals to Newcastle' because our roses in the garden here are really rather lovely, especially the trellis by the coal bunker which has a mass of pink blossoms with lots of deeper pink buds. It seems to have more and more blooms every day and it is truly glorious and smells heavenly, I wish you could see it.

You wouldn't want to see the rats' nest under the coal bunker, a dreadful discovery, but the council are coming to sort that out!

I'm on my own in the house and Pee-nuts keeps coming to distract me, so if you see any paw marks you know who is to blame. Pee-nuts is mad as a hatter and generally getting on everyone's nerves. He doesn't worry me too much, but the others can't stand him. I think the row you forecast is brewing.

Gill starts night duty tonight and Liz and Angie are away for the weekend so life is very quiet. Rita has a new lease of life, is buying new clothes and getting all dolled up. Funny, we thought. Her little houseman is back on the scene and working on the same ward as her.

The May Ball photo has arrived. I love it because we look exactly as we were, nicely sozzled at four o'clock in the morning. There's a wicked twinkle in your eye and I look as if I'm saying, "Don't you dare!"

I was not overly keen on theatres to start with and found it all a bit of a bore: clean, clean, clean and stand, stand, stand. For the first few days I had the most appalling headache and felt so tired the whole time. I think it was the accumulation of working longer hours, no daylight, all the new things to learn, remembering how to do things correctly, the general tension of theatre work and the stuffy atmosphere. I am missing you too. Tuesday night it all got too much; my head was throbbing and the others wouldn't take the hint and get on and use the bathroom so that I could have a peaceful period of relaxation in the tub. I think they were oblivious to how lousy I felt and ignored my pleas. By the time I did sink into the bath something just snapped inside and silent tears ran uncontrollably down my face. I felt alone, lonely and terribly miserable. Having got it all out of my system I took some aspirin, slept like a baby and I've been fine ever since.

Theatres are OK actually. The seniors are very helpful and kind and I'm learning new things every day. When you can see what the surgeons are doing the operations are very interesting, but some of the neuro (brain) ops go on for ages, five or six hours, and it is difficult to see anything and becomes extremely tedious. The ortho (bones) is better as it's possible to see and the cases are quicker. It makes me want to laugh when the hammers and chisels come out. A standard ortho set contains: a large hammer, small hammer, pair of pliers, screwdrivers and screws! I don't much like the grating of bones: it sets my teeth on edge, and amputations are a bit gruesome.

Yesterday we went up to Main Theatres at the Old Site to watch some general surgery, which was great because we were simply onlookers and didn't have to worry about what to do next. The first 'on call' I have to do is on Saturday night – Saturday of all days. It's bad luck, but I'm trying to convince myself there is no need to get anxious about it.

It's possible the landlady is getting a new settee instead of having this one re-covered after the water damage, and so we shall have two, hoorah! Did she guess how much in demand this one is?

Continued:

5th July 1969

I told Gill not to wake me up when she comes in off nights unless there was a letter from you. I came to with her saying, "Does a postcard count?" Of course it did. Anything from you is worth waking up for.

I've finished making my housecoat and altering a dress, and tomorrow I shall pick up the knitting needles. I've started an intensive course of exercises designed to flatten my tum so that I'll look good in a bikini.

Geoff is coming to stay which should be fun. He has a holiday job at the Ida Darwin Hospital.

It is late now and I'm writing this in bed. I think of you and feel very close to you. I think about us, past, present and future, and I daydream blissfully and try to remember all the things I want to discuss with you. Peter, I love you very, very much and the knowledge of your love for me is the most precious thing I possess.

Geoff, my middle brother, was keen to do a challenging holiday job and I suggested he worked at the Ida Darwin, a hospital cum care home for severely disabled children. It was situated close to Fulbourn and I had been there on a day visit. I was profoundly disturbed to discover society's rejects, children and young adults that I had no idea existed, hidden away. I had a huge admiration for the staff that cared for them with love and kindness. If Geoff wanted to test his emotional strength, this had to be the place.

Continued:

6th July 1969

Geoff arrived. It was super having his company and we explored the less touristy colleges, many of which I had never been into before. Corpus Christi has the most beautiful Old Court. I took him to see Churchill for a modern contrast and it felt very strange being there without you. We walked up to the chapel as I always feel drawn towards it, such an unassuming place to exude an aura of peace and tranquillity. I know you think it looks like workmen's loos from the outside, but inside I've always felt we meet on common ground despite our different religious backgrounds. I love the huge plain glass window behind the font that looks out on the natural copse of trees, simple but spiritual.

I thought I'd get used to missing you, but tonight it feels worse than ever before and it seems ages until I can be with you again. I love you and feel I ought to be with you and not here on my own. But so long as I know you love me (and believe me, I do know it) I can cope with anything. I love you and I always will.

Continued:

My goodness, what a day!

First we had a liver transplant; we dealt with the donor. That meant the scheduled list ran late, but there was a fascinating operation when surgeons opened a chap up from front to back, removed one rib, made a huge hole and collapsed one lung so they could work on the spine. The consultant let us go up close to look and we could see the heart and the other lung working. It was brilliant. Then what should happen but an emergency. This turned out to be a ruptured spleen with a torn liver and hepatic artery. Poor man: a car smash. Once they opened him up there was blood everywhere. We pumped 12 pints in, literally (I was turning the handle on the pump), which was all the available fresh blood. I don't think he will pull through. The operation was technically successful, but his condition was very, very poor. It was amazingly dramatic, and for the first time I enjoyed being in theatre. Everyone was united doing everything possible to save a life against all the odds. That is the sort of challenge I like and it was exhilarating working as a team with all the stupid protocol and status forgotten; people simply doing their utmost. I'll say a prayer for him.

Continued:

Thank you, Darling, for the postcard from Salzburg which made me wish more than anything that I could be with you. Salzburg and Vienna are places I can only dream about; I like to imagine you holding me close as we dance a Viennese waltz in a candlelit and mirrored ballroom, gloriously romantic.

Back in the real world, I've bought the wool and started knitting. Question is will you get back before I finish the jumper for you? The weather remains overcast, grey, rainy and miserable. No chance of getting a tan here. We are going to the cinema. Far from the Madding Crowd is on again; we've all seen it before, but it's a brilliant film and will make for a relaxing evening out.

Angie got called out for kidneys the other night and we are expecting another liver at any minute. I just hope it happens before my on call on Saturday.

New Airmail letter:

15th July 1969

I haven't written for a few days because I worry the letter might become as boring as my life is without you.

Your degree photo has arrived with an amusing note from your father. It's comforting to have it with me when you are so far away.

Continued:

17th July 1969

Tonight I'm on call and have to sleep at the hospital. It's a bit like solitary confinement in this grotty little room, but it does have advantages: time to write in peace, a super deep hot bath en suite and the darling telephone operator is putting a call through to home for me. He can interrupt it if there is an emergency, which there may well be as the Prof is after some kidneys and, more urgently, a liver. Still I didn't get called Saturday night and my luck may hold for tonight too.

If it was possible to buy clocks with sirens for the alarm I'd wake up in a flash. A fire engine went past the house the other morning and I nearly fell out of bed! Gill thought it was hilariously funny.

Eileen aged 18

First day in uniform

Spring at the Old Site

The Hospital Revue – Puss in Surgical Boots 1968

Puss in Surgical Boots – Eileen in front of the chorus line

Peter and Eileen at the May Ball
June 1969

Peter with his parents on Graduation Day

Peter and Eileen on Graduation Day

Eileen's 21st Birthday
Eileen, Peter, Malcolm, Geoff, Paul, Liz,
Mother, Father, Sis

Eileen in her third year with an
orderly on Griffith Ward

Eileen with Paul and Liz after
their wedding ceremony

Peter and Eileen with Canon Duckworth on their wedding day

Peter and Eileen

*Peter and Eileen Celebrating with their Cambridge Friends
Annie, Nigel, Rita, Angie, Peter, Eileen, Henry, Gill,
Ros, Steve, Alan, Dawn, Paul, Liz*

*Children's Ward with grass play area outside –
empty and awaiting demolition*

*General Nursing Council –
State Registered Nurse*

Hospital Badge

An ambulance with police escort has just whizzed in so I guess that is the end of my bath and peaceful night. Of course it may be an overdose that survives and gets sent to the Old Site. Anyway I think I'll stay dressed for a while in case.

Liz is longing to see Paul; one weekend apart nearly killed her. Angie is all lovey-dovey and Gill is in ecstasies having Henry back. Rita is depressed again. I feel sorry for her surrounded by all of us in love; it rather emphasises her aloneness.

It's nearly an hour since the ambulance arrived and the phone has not rung so I think I'll risk a quick bath. You can bet I'll get called the minute I'm soaking wet.

Miracles never cease. I've had a lovely long bath and no interruption. I must be one of the luckiest people alive. I've known that ever since I met you. I'll get into bed and sleep with my fingers crossed. Night-night.

Continued:

19th July 1969

Travelling home I had to stand all the way into London, and again out the other side. Thank goodness they were express trains as my feet were killing me after a busy day at work.

I wonder if you realised we have been together for six months now.

Everyone is having a good time. I enjoyed my days off at home and had fun in Cambridge with my parents when they gave me a lift back. We went canoeing on the Cam as there were long queues for the punts. Rita is in seventh heaven because the houseman she fancies talks to her. The weather is glorious, typical when I'm working all day every day. At the weekend it was really quiet in theatres and we got all the cleaning done in record time and took turns to sunbathe on the roof. There is a hatch to get up there and a parapet around the edge so if we crawl and then lie flat we can't be seen. It felt a bit naughty, but wasn't doing any harm, so why not?

I'm up to the armholes on the back of your jumper already, how's that for progress?

Sending all my love, my thoughts are always of you and I'm glad you are having a wonderful time. I'm writing this in bed wearing my sexy nightie, the one I wore to the pyjama party, only this time with rather less on underneath! I'm so overflowing with love for you I shall have to send you bucketfuls else I shall be at risk of drowning. Only you can save me.

Continued:

21st July 1969

Man has landed on the moon! I'm afraid this significant moment rather passed me by in a blur of work and sleep. I find it difficult to comprehend how amazing it is supposed to be. Exactly what difference does it make to mankind? Compared to pioneering medicine and surgery, or feeding the starving, I think it is a waste of money and fail to understand what all the fuss is about.

Continued:

27th July 1969

Here I am once again in the on call room. My luck so far is all a bit too good to be true, and on the law of averages I'm bound to be busy tonight. I do wish cars would stop screeching into Accident Service as I have to keep leaping up to look out of the window. That one was a Black Maria with a drunk inside to judge from the singing.

Parents have said Geoff can borrow the car whilst they are away on holiday which is rather super. At the house things are pretty dull because Gill, Liz and Rita are all on nights and Angie and I have completely opposite shifts. (Oh goodness, now there are two ambulances and a Black Maria. I wish I hadn't looked. The sirens weren't going, thinks she hopefully.)

I really must go to sleep, though it is horribly hot in this little cell and I shall be frizzled up by morning.

Another Airmail letter:

30th July 1969

There is very little news, but having heard from you I feel I can write cheerfully about nothing instead of miserably about missing you. I can feel your love pouring out of the letter and it is strong and faithful even across all these miles.

I went out to the Ida Darwin Hospital to visit Geoff whilst he was working. I know the charge nurse; I worked with him when he did his general training at Addenbrooke's and it was good to see him again. I got roped in to help with the ward routine, but I didn't mind a bit. Some of the children stare vacantly into space, but others are really rather loveable when you look beyond their hideous physical appearance. In contrast one little baby girl had the most beautiful face I have ever seen. She could have been a very expensive porcelain doll: black curly hair, long eyelashes, a pink and white complexion, a sweet little button nose and cupid bow lips. But exactly like a doll there is no life in her eyes and her limbs are floppy. I found it heartbreaking that a seemingly perfect child can be alive but not live. Like me, Geoff had no idea so many children are shut away where most people will never see them, but he is finding the work very rewarding.

We had another ruptured spleen in yesterday. Three on consecutive Tuesdays, and I've been on duty for all of them. Isn't that a coincidence? It was real life drama again. A big car smash in Bottisham, three killed, one almost dead (a probable kidney/liver donor) and the other is the luckiest man alive. He was trapped in his car by his feet and had ruptured his spleen and gut. He was in a bad way when we got him, but the operation went smoothly – we've had lots of practice – and we sent him on to Gill's loving care on night duty.

This morning I popped in to see Gill on my way upstairs and stopped to say hello to him. He is fine now, and it felt fantastic to know I was there and had helped to save his life.

It makes all those long days of boring routine worthwhile. Suddenly I realised theatre staff never get thanked as the patients are inevitably asleep and never see them again. That's sad.

Continued:

Over half way through our separation now and in some ways time has flown by. It seems impossible that I've nearly finished on theatres and all that appeared daunting at the start is second nature to me now, even if I am still nervous of autoclaves.

All this evening Liz and I have been in fits of giggles. She smashed her specs, and whilst they are being mended she is wearing 'National Healths'. If I look at her I collapse laughing.

My day off has been busy with washing, cleaning the kitchen (even defrosted the fridge), writing letters, knitting some more of your jumper and I spent the middle part of the day with Mother who had come to visit, which was a lovely surprise. It was more exhausting than a day working.

Continued:

Bad news today, we've still got to do a practical exam with our finals. Damn! On top of that I was told I am being sent to Main Theatres next week, if you please, because they are short staffed. It is the most ludicrous and stupid thing I have ever heard. Main Theatres are completely different from the New Site and they do even the most basic things by different methods. I shan't know where anything is kept and shall be more of a hindrance than a help. Even more annoying is that a nurse has just come to us from there. Why not send her back? Surely that would be the logical thing to do because she knows the routine and could help more. I am so cross; Sister didn't ask me nicely, just told me. I'm feeling insecure and miserable at the prospect, especially as I was starting to feel confident and enjoy New Site Theatres. Petty occurrences like this make me want to shout and yell at them all, run away and never come back. This morning I was happy, and then all this happens. I suppose I'll pull through, I always do.

Main theatres was very different, but Liz was there and helped me, except when we were cleaning and she soaked my feet with a bucketful of water, forgetting that I had white plimsolls on and not the wellies the nurses wear at the Old Site! In many ways I was lucky to experience the contrasting methods and different operations in both theatres. I was relieved there were no abortions that week in Main Theatres as I found the idea of destroying a normal foetus abhorrent. I believed reliable contraception should be made more widely available, and used, to prevent unwanted pregnancies.

New letter:

10th August 1969

I've just come back from church and we start Red Block tomorrow. I hope the lectures are interesting. Gill has promised to sit beside me to ensure I stay awake. What would I do without her? She's so reliable.

Angie and I went to see Chitty Chitty Bang Bang. It is a beautiful children's film and it was relaxing to slip into a fantasy world right up to the 'lived happily ever after'.

The latest progress report is that I am half way up the front of the jumper, have finished making a beach robe and completed my patient study. I've started cutting out some little dresses from remnants for my Goddaughter for her birthday in November. They will look very cute.

Thank you for the depth you have given to my life and the beauty of love that I continue to experience day by day despite you being so far away. Most valuable are all the hopes and promises for a heavenly future together. I pray I'll make you the happiest husband in the world, and maybe one day a proud father too!

Continued:

I'm sure I spend too much time thinking of you when I should be concentrating on lectures. I miss you so much. I thought it would get easier as time passes, but it doesn't and the time seems to go slower as your return gets nearer. Roll on the day when I am in your arms again. If I'm honest my life is not miserable without you, but it does feel empty compared to when you are here.

Thank you for your lovely long letters, they have all meant a great deal to me. One of them arrived at 7am on Saturday and the postman rang to demand four pence postage and woke Gill up. She says she has forgiven you, but won't forgive Liz and Angie who lay in bed wide awake and didn't attempt to go to answer the door. Needless to say I didn't hear a thing until Gill crashed back into the bedroom cursing us all.

The weather is foul and I've retreated into winter woollies and my new pair of flared cords.

Block is over half way through already, thank goodness. One can have too much of all female company. As usual the lectures are repetitive, boring and monotonous. The first week I kept falling asleep, which was a bit embarrassing as I'm sitting at the front. We employed all sorts of tactics to keep me awake and now have a patent system. Gill (beside me) winks at Dawn (behind me) who prods me in the back with her ruler and I come to for another couple of minutes if we're lucky.

Yesterday we went out with the district nurses. It was very different to nursing in the hospital. The first lady we visited was elderly and bedridden. I gave her a bed bath whilst the district nurse talked to her equally elderly sister who lived with her and looked after her. When we were back in the car I asked what was wrong with her because I hadn't picked up on a diagnosis. The answer was most bizarre: apparently her fiancé died in the First World War when she was eighteen and she took to her bed and hasn't got up since and her sister has cared for her all that time. I don't think I'd have that much patience.

Stop press news: Liz and Paul are buying the ring this Saturday and then going to see Parents to break the news. Paul spoke to Liz's dad last weekend. Just imagine, she'll be my sister-in-law!

Rita has adopted a new tactic: if we get too ratty with the cat she says she'll have it put to sleep. We might not love the animal, but she knows we wouldn't have it killed. We've been to see Dr Doolittle and The Love Bug, which was absolutely hilarious. We laughed and laughed. Tonight we are going to see Dr Zhivago again because I need a little romance in my life whilst you are away. Rita isn't coming and dared to say the reason was because love isn't a bit like it is portrayed in the film, not half so beautiful. I felt really sorry for her because, definitely, love is the most beautiful thing in the world, and since I've known you I truly believe that. I hope Rita is as lucky as me one day.

The knitting circle has grown. Rita has started a scarf, Liz is sewing up the Arran jumper she knitted for Paul, Gill is finishing the edging on Henry's cardigan and I'm doing the button holes for her. As for your jumper, I win the bet: it will be finished this coming weekend.

Trying to look as if I'm taking notes, I have been writing this in a pharmacology lecture and now in an equally boring one on dietetics. Good news: I've got Bank Holiday Monday off. The tutors have been decent and made it a study day, though I doubt any of us will be doing that. As you get back on Sunday is there any chance of seeing you? I'm trying not to build my hopes up in case it is not possible. Longing with all my heart for your return, hearing your voice, seeing you, getting real kisses and being back where I belong.

Paul and Liz became engaged, with much celebration, on 30th August.

Peter returned from Europe and came to see me on 6th

September. Reunited, but with little money between us, we went to stay with my Godmother for a week in Jersey, Channel Islands, where I had spent many a happy summer when I was a child. She was very generous, fed us well, lent us her car and assumed we'd want to be alone. She was right!

23rd September 1969

Darling Peter,

Shattered I am, completely shattered. Monday I came back from work and collapsed into bed, Tuesday I came back with a splitting headache, slept all afternoon and went to bed early, and I've been asleep again this afternoon. I'm so tired, and sleeping is such a waste of time. I wish we were still on holiday and I was seeing you every day. Night duty will be very welcome as it is less hectic.

I love being on Children's Ward. We've got a sad little girl in who is crippled with rheumatoid arthritis and has a big moon face from the steroids. I had thought only old people got arthritis. The pain is horrible, but she is very accepting of her condition and is impressively brave. She loves the Polyphon. This is a giant musical box, a huge contraption in a glass case which plays enormous, heavy brass discs that are anchored in vertically instead of horizontally. It is the most marvellous distraction for distressed children, and their parents too. I love the cheerful sound it makes.

The good news is we all passed, except Liz – oops! I came top of our household and fourth in the set. We have to go to see Matron to get our third year belts.

Apparently Henry has decided when he and Gill will get engaged, but won't tell her. Liz is thinking about transferring to Hereford to be near Paul and finishing her training there. I hope she doesn't as it will make the house more expensive for the other four of us and wouldn't be as good a qualification for her. Rita has gone off her houseman. Unfortunately Pee-nuts arrived back from a stay with Rita's family: we had hoped he'd gone for good.

The hospital is in chaos. Apparently sixty people are off sick with depression and one girl has attempted suicide. Also seventy nurses handed in their notice last month so something is very wrong somewhere. Every ward is desperately short staffed, and Liz found herself looking after twenty-six patients on Ward 2 completely on her own for a full shift. It is ridiculous as we are all overworked, overtired, stressed and frustrated. Such is the life of a student nurse.

A few days after this letter was written Peenuts was hit by a car and was found dead beside the main road outside The Nursery. None of us would have wished this to happen, but it did solve the problem!

Autumn 1969 saw the start of a 'flu epidemic that went on all winter and seriously affected both staffing levels and morale at the hospital.

Third Year

29th September 1969

Darling Peter,

The best moment of night duty is coming home and finding a lovely, long letter from you, being able to go to bed reading it and fall asleep very happy. This morning I went to get my third year purple belt and a quick halo polish from Matron. I wish I could have caught it on tape as nobody, but nobody else, sings my praises like that. Load of twaddle, but it made me feel like the cat's whiskers.

As for night duty, after phoning you I was seriously sick, but then felt decidedly better, staggered to work and somehow got through the night on a diet of Lucozade, which tastes disgusting. Saturday and Sunday nights I was senior (ha! ha!) because everyone else has gone off sick and I've had to cope with help from other wards. Fortunately it has been relatively quiet. The first night a baby girl, nine days old, went suddenly and inexplicably ashen grey/blue. Help! Then last night it got busy as our littlest baby in an incubator was very dodgy and Night Sister spent half the night on the ward with me as we tried our best to improve the poor mite's condition. We had to call the doc in, phone the consultant, X-rays, the lot. My tea-break, when I was going to write to you, never happened. I'm sorry, Darling, but it looks like babies are coming between us already! I can tell you there have been some frightening moments; children get seriously ill very quickly. Apart from that I love being on Children's Ward and especially on night duty. I love feeding and bathing the babies. I think I was born for this role; they are so cuddly and kissable I can feel positively broody.

Peter started working for International Computers Limited and spent his initial training period at Moor Hall, Cookham. Then he was posted to the Sheffield office as a systems' engineer. This meant we could only see each other at weekends, when of course I was often working.

Letter home:

7th October 1969

This is the first chance I've had to write home since my holiday. I'm on night duty. The first two nights passed quickly, and although busy we managed quite well. The third night saw muggins here in charge, but fortunately the ward was quiet and the babies good; we even had time for a few secret rides on the rocking horse! It was all a tad daunting. I had a nurse from the set below us as my middle and she was very helpful at keeping me calm, but that was her last night. The junior is a first year, just, and an efficient worker, but rather slow and scared stiff of babies. Night Sister was super and answered a million questions. She was aware I had only just got my third year belt; I wasn't going to wear it for fear it would be assumed I had more knowledge than I have, but she insisted I put it on. She was very supportive.

"Now if anything, anything at all, however slight, worries you then page me. I shall probably say 'Knickers', but I'll tell you to your face if I think you are making an unnecessary fuss, so don't worry. If in doubt, ring."

So I did. In the morning I walked in to have a quick peep at my babies, and play with one who is particularly gorgeous and full of chuckles, when I noticed another baby was lying there grey/blue and she felt all floppy when I picked her up. You've never seen me move so fast. I threw the baby at the other nurse saying "Do something" and dashed for the phone. Night Sister arrived in two seconds flat and my heart started again. The baby was fine; apparently the brain damage she had suffered at birth tends to make her go like that, and all we need to do is blow hard on her face to startle her and she'll breathe and pink up again. I wish someone had warned me.

Being in charge I had to write the report and take it down to Night Sister's office, which felt very grown up. I was pleased I had weathered the storm of my first night as senior and less daunted the next night when there was only me and the junior. (There are supposed to be three nurses on Children's Ward at night plus a staff nurse in charge.) I got sent a useless senior to help; admittedly she coped with the less ill babies, but did nothing else. I wished they had sent one of the GOS (Great Ormond Street) nurses, who are here for a year to get their general nursing qualification, because they are dab hands at feeding babies. Sometimes they appear in their break to have a cuddle and are only too pleased to lend a hand, but this never seems to happen when we are frantically busy.

That night the saga of Nurse Walker getting much too involved with her patient began. We had a six-day-old baby girl who was very seriously ill in an incubator. She was born with her wind and food pipe joined (tracheoesophageal fistula) and part of her food pipe was missing too. I had already specialled her on day duty as she had undergone two extensive operations, the second one a repeat as the first repair broke down. She had been making steady progress, but that night she got worse and we had to call the doctors and the X-ray girl. I ended up in the cubicle specialling her and trying to run the ward at the same time. We managed somehow and Night Sister was brilliant: kept popping in and out to check I was coping. The next night I got another nurse from our set to help, which was fantastic, especially as the baby had gone to theatre again. She returned in the middle of the night and the other nurse had to special her whilst I looked after the other babies and kept an eye on the junior in the ward. Even so I had to keep going in to give a hand with drips, numerous drainage tubes and feeding tubes. Night Sister came at dawn to help and we left that baby in a really good condition in a spotless incubator in a tidy cubicle. Sister had us on our knees scrubbing the floor! We all felt very pleased with ourselves, and somehow the tiredness and lack of breaks didn't matter.

The next night there was simply me and the junior again, which seemed ridiculous. This made more sense when I took report and learnt the baby's condition had deteriorated and the doctors could do no more. All the tubes were removed and the baby couldn't be fed as the intestine was in spasm. It was a sentence to starvation, and it was gut-wrenching because outwardly she looked a perfect baby. To hear her crying because she was lonely and hungry was heartbreaking. It is the most difficult thing I've encountered so far and it seems so sad that neither of her parents was here. I looked after her all night as the junior was too emotional. It upset me too: I knew I'd grown much too fond of her as I'd helped her fight for life ever since I started on the ward. I spent all the time I could with her, cuddling her, praying for her and doing all I could to help her.

Sister was a star. She called the doctors and got permission for us to keep the baby heavily sedated; that was all we could do. Last night, amazingly, she was still alive. Night Sister had realised I was too involved and ordered me not to go into the cubicle and she would come at regular intervals and care for the baby herself. Needless to say on one of those visits she caught me in there. Well, could you sit at a desk knowing a baby was suffering alone nearby and not go and be with her?

Night Sister and I formed quite a bond that night. We talked about religion and euthanasia and she reassured me that she has been too involved with patients at times too. She even offered me a lift home. It was the last night for both of us; and I thanked her sincerely for all her help because, honestly, I couldn't have managed without her support, which she gave so kindly and willingly.

She said, "Don't mention it. It was a pleasure to work with you." That meant a lot after some pretty gruelling nights.

But the baby had still not died. I suffered all day worrying about her; it was silly, but I couldn't get her out of my mind. We went to see Oliver in the evening, which is a beautiful film, but all the time I was thinking about that baby. I could not cycle home without stopping as we got to the hospital; an invisible thread was pulling me towards the ward.

Staff Nurse was in charge and she didn't mind me calling in. When I asked after the baby, the junior said, "I knew you'd be back."

Staff Nurse said, "Go and see her" which surprised me as I was in ordinary clothes. I didn't need telling twice and, what a surprise, it was wonderful. Her condition had resolved to the extent that they could start feeding her again; admittedly straight into the small intestine, and her oesophagus was still a mess, but it was fantastic progress. The odds were still against her as she had developed pneumonia, but at least she stood a chance and wasn't hungry. What a fighter.

She died at the weekend. Peter was here and we had a perfect time doing nothing much as we can't afford to go out at present. It was the best thing as I needed some peace and quiet and love more than anything. I shall never forget that baby.

11th October 1969

Darling Peter,

Sister had to put me on nights again as there is no other senior to go on and I only just qualify.

One of the technicians from New Site Theatres appeared at the house on Wednesday. He is from Mauritius and apparently it was the fourth time he had called and the first time he had found me at home. I hastened to explain that I am seeing you as much as possible. He took the hint and only stayed for a quick cuppa to save face and then left. He is sweet and amusing and I would love to visit his homeland one day, but I don't want to go out with him. I've got you.

We are busy with lots of babies. Each time we go into a different baby cubicle we have to wash our hands and put on a long-sleeved ankle length white gown (much like a theatre gown) and sometimes a mask as well. It is time consuming, but necessary to prevent cross infection. Already I am a dab hand at folding kite shaped nappies for girls and triangular ones for boys and proudly wear a string of nappy pins dangling from my breast pocket. (The badge of honour that proclaims I am working on Children's Ward.) All the babies wear long white hospital nighties and look angelic, but some of them are slow feeders and can't be hurried. Successfully feeding a baby with a hare lip and cleft palate is a skill and demands a lot of patience. We get fond of their funny faces and, thank goodness, most of them can be efficiently repaired nowadays. A toddler was admitted with croup tonight and I had to set up the oxygen tent on my own for the first time; amazing how quickly it cured the problem.

I've started to knit a cardigan for my Goddaughter to go with the little dresses and hope to get it finished on night duty.

16th October 1969

I'm sorry I sounded miserable on the phone, but you know what I'm like. I'll try to explain why I had to go on nights again. Obviously you need to have seniors and juniors to cover the work. If there are lots of seniors on the ward then that is fine because they can easily cover the junior's workload, but conversely the juniors cannot do senior duties because they have not got the training nor the experience. Three of our seniors are off sick and those of us left have to cover. I need you to understand it is not a matter of choice. I'm thinking positively because the more nights I do the more often I get a whole weekend off to see you. Anyway, to be honest, I prefer nights and Night Sister is teaching me so much more than I would get to learn on day duty. I like being in charge when I have time to read up the case histories, do things the right way and run the ward in my own style. This includes the best thing of all, which is being able to play with the children in the morning without Sister watching disapprovingly. I am convinced play is as important in their recovery as medicine. For instance, we have a little boy who is four years old and has cystic fibrosis (a lung condition). He was very difficult, stroppy and refusing to take his medicine. In the end I had to pass a nasogastric tube to get his drugs and food into him, which he accepted surprisingly well. Now he is getting better and is happy and smiling and loves to play, when he is not putting up with the physio pummelling his chest at regular intervals. He used to scream when he saw me coming, but we are now the best of friends. As his prognosis is not good and he is bound to have to come in again, I think it is important that he takes happy memories home with him and will not be so scared next time.

In the bed alongside him is a cheeky little chap who is a bit older. He slipped his mother's hand and ran into the road coming home from school. He was run over by a lorry with the wheel crushing his pelvis and the internal organs. The pelvis has been pieced back together and the organs sorted: fortunately the bladder wasn't ruptured, but he had to have a colostomy as his large bowel was beyond repair. The biggest problem now is the large skin grafts which are reluctant to heal. He will be in for a long, long time and we are all very fond of him.

I have a horribly painful sore throat and am losing my voice. I can't afford to go off sick (they might put me down a set and then I couldn't take finals with my friends) and am taking a self-prescribed course of penicillin which should work brilliantly. My voice is very deep and the others tease me that it sounds sexy.

27th October 1969

I've arrived back at The Nursery having worked at least an hour overtime. I feel thoroughly exhausted and I suppose I'm a mug not to walk off at the end of my shift and leave the others to it. We had two more babies admitted making us frantically busy again, and I won't leave until everything is in order. I've got feeding babies down to a fine art.

I'm going on night duty again on Sunday next, which has the bonus I can spend the whole of the day with you. Isn't that perfect? Sister did apologise for putting me on again so soon.

It's another beautiful day today and has been a wonderful autumn so far. The problem is the leaves are looking at me and saying "Come and sweep us up" and I really have not got the energy.

Will you wear a dinner jacket for my twenty-first birthday party? You'd look super, very smart, and it would be perfect alongside the new evening dress I'm making. Please, for me?

It's pay day on Thursday, which is lucky as I'm nearly at the end of the notepad again and this is the last envelope.

Letter home:
30th October 1969

Pay day, hoorah! I was too broke to phone, and we've got our third year rise too. I earn a grand total of £40 a month now, even if I only see £32 of it.

I've sent out the invitations to my twenty-first party and I enclose the list. I should explain that most of the nurses won't be able to reply until the week before when they get their off duty rota. It is very unlikely all ten will make it, but we are keeping our fingers crossed. I'm on the change list today to go to Ground Floor, Douglas House (that's where the Prof does his transplants), but my ward is minor surgery: hernias, bunions and such like. I'll be there over my twenty-first and time off shouldn't be a problem, especially as they do Thurs–Thurs nights and that would work well. I can finish nights on the morning of my birthday and have that day and the whole weekend off; must be a snag somewhere, it sounds too good to be true.

Peter came up last weekend and we had a super time, except

I keep coming off duty late which he doesn't understand and finds very annoying. We took advantage of Henry's new room at Selwyn to watch the rugby. It's like being in a box, watching them play outside in the cold east wind and us inside, cosy and warm. It turned into a spontaneous party which was the best fun.

The ward is absolutely chaotic and the new PTS set has started, which doesn't help. I've been working flat out: babies, babies and, would you believe, more babies. I love it, but I shall be on nights for 5th November so you can think of me. We've already had three children in with firework injuries and it is not funny. I can assure you I shall keep my children well away from fireworks having seen what can happen.

3rd November 1969

Darling Peter,

The pianist and composer of the Hospital Revue has been chatting me up. He's got some super ideas for lots of dancing and wants me to do the choreography. I'm keen to accept the challenge and feel honoured to have been asked. I am confident I can do it; besides it will be fun. Gill has promised to help me and they have asked Rita to be the female lead. Which doctor will play opposite her is undecided; I hope he can dance! Although it will absorb all my spare time until Christmas, I am sure it will be worth it. Of course I can fix rehearsals to suit me which will be great, and I hope Annie and several others from last year's chorus line will be in it again. This year it is called Jack and Pill and the script is hilarious. It won't interfere with me seeing you at all, but you'll absolutely have to come to the last night and the party afterwards.

Rita's new man has been round again – very keen, don't you think? She cooked him baked beans, how romantic!

5th November 1969

Thank you for phoning me tonight. I wish I knew what to say to comfort you now your grandmother has died. For all my nursing experience of dealing with death, one thing always floors me and that is what to say to the grieving relatives. Words seem either pathetic or trite, and yet how else can I communicate my sympathy when we are apart? Believe me it is beautiful to see someone at peace after they've been ill for a long time, and I personally find it a comfort to know that at last they have no worries, nor pain, and are surrounded by loving thoughts. I want to hold you in my arms and kiss the hurt away. In a way it is sad she never knew about me and us, but on the other hand she has never had the worry of me not being Jewish. We've been so close these last two weekends and so very, very happy that it hurts me to think of you feeling sad now. I'm close by you in thought and love you very much.

7th November 1969

Sorry I was rushed on the telephone last night, but it was all happening: a liver transplant, what else? I had to gulp my supper down and get back to prepare for the fray. Originally I was going to special this precious little lad, but Night Sister decided to send a Great Ormond Street nurse down from one of the other wards. It was a pity not to be looking after him, but made sense that I ran the rest of the ward as I know the patients. I may well be the one to special him tonight; just imagine, the first child to have a liver transplant, it's so exciting! Of course this is all very hush, hush, so don't breathe a word to anyone. I had to tell you to explain my abruptness, and because it is too thrilling not to share.

Written from my parents' house:
11th November 1969

My Dearest Darling Peter,

Mother is taking me back to Cambridge tomorrow morning, which means we can take lots of wood to help keep The Nursery warm. Sadly I've got an awful cold. I hope it goes soon as I dare not be ill again.

I'm looking forward to seeing you at the weekend, but

can't promise to be at the station to meet you because I still don't know my off duty. Sister can't promise anything because of the present state of drama over the liver transplant and the necessity for seniors to special the little boy. I'll pull all the strings I can, but if I'm not there then come to The Nursery and I'll have left a note for you.

I delivered my Goddaughter's presents (and her mum's twenty-first gift) this evening in time to play with her before she went to bed. She is gorgeous, full of giggles, and has learnt how to climb on and off the settee.

Yes, you're right: Mother is dropping hints about us getting engaged. You should never have asked for my opinion because honestly it is your prerogative to choose the moment. If we get engaged sooner then we wouldn't be continually trying to hold back, fighting emotion with logical arguments that aren't really convincing either of us. Are we scared a long engagement would spoil the beauty of it? It couldn't. Are we frightened of extra strain on the relationship? No. Do we think things would grow stale? How could they? I could continue for pages, but I love you and I am yours anyway so the timing is up to you. I haven't mentioned my hopes or thoughts to anyone else, and shan't because this is a special matter between us alone.

Sadly the little boy who had the liver transplant died. Without it he could only have lived a few short weeks more anyway. I worried his parents were given false hope, but know they were fully informed and I witnessed their courage. Without these, and other brave people, medicine could not progress.

20th November 1969

Darling Peter,

Work on the revue continues to take up all my spare time. Gill is being her usual helpful self with the choreography, and Annie plus Lala, another girl from our set, are definitely in the chorus line. I am all ready for the first rehearsal tonight. Two dancers have dropped out and I'm searching for likely replacements. I think the others are sick of hearing the music as I play the tape over and over again. I'm working on the opening number, which must be 'razzle-dazzle' as it sets the mood for the whole show. I've finished one more elegant dance routine and have clear ideas on how the rest will work. Rita is loving being principal lady and approves of her leading man. I'm choreographing a tango for them. Best of all, I've managed to avoid having rehearsals whenever I am seeing you: after all, the revue is a passing phase and you are a permanent fixture in my life, and a very nice one too!

Ground Floor, Douglas House, must have been designed as a rest cure for tired nurses. At the minute this is perfect. There is absolutely nothing to do except serve meals and bandage the odd leg. The highlights of the week are a few very minor operations. All this is fine when I'm in charge, but Sister expects us all to be busy when she is here and pretending is exhausting. I hear night duty consists of brewing cups of tea and trying to stay awake. I shall buy some more wool this afternoon to be prepared.

I do miss the children.

I wish I was seeing you this weekend and could be near you. You sounded sad and lonely on the phone and I want to hold you tight and tell you how much I love you. Would that help?

24th November 1969

The nights are very long as there is so little to do, Friday seems an age away. I've got loads of knitting done and letters written, but I'd much rather be busy nursing. Funny how when we are rushed off our feet we yearn for peace and tranquillity, but when we get it we are bored.

One of my teeth has an exposed nerve and it is horribly painful if I bite on it. I'll have to make a flying visit home to see the dentist and then I'll miss the candlelit service at Great St Mary's Church this Sunday, which is a pity as I love it and it always makes Christmas seem very close.

Thank goodness it is pay day on Thursday. I intend to cook a slap up meal for when you get here on Friday and make a real fuss of you with lots and lots of cuddles.

2nd December 1969

I returned to Cambridge feeling on top of the world, and the feeling persists despite efforts to dampen it. The dentist struck with a vengeance, but filled an upper front tooth as well for no extra charge, which was a bonus.

Today and tomorrow I am to help on Middle Floor, which is skin diseases. What I've done to deserve this I fail to comprehend and Sister claims I am working two hours less time than I should. I am certain that is not true, but suppose I'll have to keep my big mouth shut, do the extra, and count my blessings I've got the off duty I wanted for my twenty-first. Plans are well advanced for the party, but Liz, oh dear, has got German measles. Keep your fingers crossed we don't all catch it as I do not fancy being all spotty on my big day!

Don't let thoughts of us being apart at Christmas upset you. We can have the most wonderful, marvellous, scrumptious, merry Christmases in our future together. I love you more than words can express, more than a letter can tell and with all my heart. I do so love you.

I became an adult, and eligible to vote, on my twenty-first birthday, 11th December 1969. It was my last morning on night duty and the patients made a fuss of me with an enormous card they had all signed and a huge box of chocolates. Mother came to collect me and we drove home to prepare for my party on the Saturday. My parents were experts at throwing a perfect party, and their house lent itself to large gatherings with a parquet floor in a huge square hall for dancing, a lounge and morning room for sitting and chatting and a large dining room for the buffet. There was music and dancing, plenty of delicious food and drink, laughter and love. All my family was there, friends from school and Cambridge, and old family friends too. At midnight the corks popped on the Asti Spumante (we couldn't afford champagne), there were toasts and speeches and I blew the candles out on a giant coffee and walnut cake that Mother had made and decorated with items to reflect my favourite things, including photographs of Peter and my Goddaughter. When my brother Paul turned twenty-one his party had fallen on the day of my seventeenth birthday; this time my party was on his twenty-fifth birthday, and he had a chocolate cake. Several friends stayed the night and my bedroom became the girls' dormitory, with the boys sleeping in my two brothers' rooms. I loved being the centre of attention for one very special evening.

15th December 1969

Darling Peter,

I've had to scrounge notepaper, envelope and stamp from the patients to write this. Life is hectic enough anyway and a Nurses' Rep. Council meeting will just about finish me off. I shall put our points across strongly, like why should those of us in the Hospital Revue have to work three hours overtime this week to get appropriate days off to be in the show? Plus, I am still unsure of my Christmas off duty, so can't make any plans. That is unfair and unnecessary.

The revue is in the exhausting stage of rehearsal when one wonders if it will ever be 'all right on the night', but I am thrilled you will be here for the Saturday performance. I'm looking for a special dress as the cast are bound to give me a bouquet on the last night and I want to look my best walking onto the stage to receive it. I've spotted a mini-dress, crocheted in white wool with a silver thread running through it, and I think it will look perfect with the silver evening shoes I wore for the May Ball.

My birthday weekend was wonderful. It was so exciting and special, and I do agree it would not have been the right moment for you to get down on one knee, even if Mother was hopeful. I know you'll choose a time fairly soon and that it will be better for being a separate celebration. I suppose we should be pleased Mother is determinedly egging us on as it shows how much she approves of you as a future son-in-law. I am longing to be with you for ever and ever.

Addenbrooke's Hospital Revue Society presented Jack and Pill at the Ley's School theatre on 18th, 19th and 20th December at 8.30pm. Tickets 6s.

The local paper said:

Groan humour at its best. Most of the gags may be old, but they are given a clever new twist.

The vocal versions of Chopin's Minute Waltz and Beethoven's Moonlight Sonata are feats of ingenuity.

A line of high step-ping chorus girls, choreographed by Eileen Walker, helped to balance the show.

This is a mindless but far from witless evening with no puns pulled. Like all good revues it is in a class entirely of its own.

It was a privilege to be involved in the show and we had so much fun. My mini-dress was greeted with cat calls and wolf whistles (or was that for my legs?) as I walked onto the stage to receive a beautiful bouquet of flowers. The tango I had choreographed so carefully became totally over exaggerated on the night and brought the house down, it was perfect and I laughed until tears streamed down my face. The after-show party was all the better for having Peter by my side.

Nursing was a big part of my life, and the hospital had become both a second home and an additional family.

26th December 1969

Darling Peter,

The most horrible thing has happened, and by the time you get this letter I expect you will have read about it in the papers. Yesterday, Christmas Day, was lovely on Ward 4 and we had a good time with the patients, including lots of jokes and banter. I was on an early shift today and we rolled up on the ward, laughing and ready to continue partying.

We were in the changing room putting on our hats when a night nurse rushed in and said, "Get that tinsel off your hats and sober up, we need you to help out here." There had been the most awful fire in the hotel in Saffron Walden and the ward was rapidly filling up with patients, though the worst of the burns cases went straight on from Accident Service to the Burns Unit at Ely. We were rushed off our feet all shift. The worst thing of all was some patients didn't know what had happened to their husband/wife/relatives, and of course we had to be suitably vague as we didn't know the specific answers, but knew several people had died. We couldn't reassure them and could only give them something for the physical pain of their broken bones. Their distress was catching and the whole episode was quite one of the most difficult things I have had to cope with. We usually feel wonderful every time we help someone, but today I came off duty feeling absolutely wrung out and heartbroken that such a horrible thing can happen. I felt so inadequate. The Christmas spirit was killed off as quickly as those poor people who had died. The thought of anything happening to you and us being separated and not knowing how the other was does not bear thinking about. I love you so very much. I wish I could end on a happy note, but I simply can't, sorry.

A Christmas night that ended in grim tragedy.

At 1.30am on Boxing Day a fire started in the television room of the Rose and Crown Hotel in Saffron Walden. It was thought to have been caused by faulty electrics in a television set. The hotel was a four storey building and there were over thirty resident guests. In total seventy-five fire-fighters and twelve appliances attended. The fire spread alarmingly quickly and easily as there were few fireproof doors and those had mostly been left open. Seventeen people were rescued. Two men slid down a roof from a third floor window into the hotel yard and others were helped by local residents using builders' ladders. Some jumped to safety sustaining multiple injuries. Eleven people died.

At the time it was the worst hotel fire in UK history and led directly to more stringent fire regulations and ultimately to The Fire Precautions Act, 1971.

30th December 1969

Darling Peter,

In another forty-eight hours it will be 1970 and then we'll be able to say "Next year we can get married." That will make it sound much closer. Thank you for giving me another wonderful weekend. I think sharing our problems brings us closer together and I love discussing our everyday experiences and our hopes for the future. I love you, Darling, more than ever and more each day, knowing you better and wanting to be closer. We are firm friends and I think that is important before we become lovers too.

As far as our sexual relationship goes, I am thinking about it. The same facts and arguments seem to churn over and over leading nowhere. I have no satisfactory answers, but it must be a problem that faces every couple. Somehow everyone must find a solution; the problem is deciding on the right one for us, and I know it will become clear eventually. Many times I want to be your mistress, but always and at all times I want to be your wife.

So many people ask me, "Why aren't you and Peter engaged?" Why? A few months back I knew the reply and I thought I knew the reasons. I was happy to wait. Suddenly, I can't remember the answers anymore. Is it simply your financial situation? I know it is your right to choose the moment and I don't even want to persuade you sooner or later. I just need to be able to answer the question convincingly.

The return to work yesterday was shattering and busier

than ever. The hospital has closed four wards altogether and is only accepting emergencies, but the existing wards are overcrowded and the nurses exhausted (nearly ninety are off sick). The situation on Ward 4 has improved; our sister is ill, but another sister from a closed ward has been sent with her staff nurses to take over. She was promoted recently and is great to work with as she is not only efficient, but says thank you!

It is very strange at The Nursery because we live together, but never seem to see each other. Liz is on nights, Gill away, Angie at home, and Rita and I are on opposite shifts. It is eerily quiet. Rumour has it Rita's leading man is taking her to Matron's Ball and borrowing his uncle's Rolls Royce Silver Ghost for the occasion. I'm happy with your new car and I think it is perfect for us. I might even help you clean it, but only in the summer! I think of it as our car because I simply can't help wanting it to be the beginning of the future – first our car and then our home. I love you, want you, need you.

1st January 1970

Good news: I've got a half day next Friday and the day off for your birthday, hoorah!

I've put my name on the list for the Hospital Ball and, fingers crossed, I can get the time off for that too. At least the Eightsome's formal twenty-first do is carefully planned for the first weekend of Blue Block so we shall all be able to go.

I feel much less tired and actually enjoyed myself these last two shifts; 1970 feels like a year full of presents waiting to be opened.

5th January 1970

Looking back through last year's diary I observed that overall we've been together many more weekends than apart. Oh, for the time when I shall see you every day again.

Work was chaotic yesterday as there was a huge pile up

involving several vehicles. There were five bodies and we had six admissions in two hours. Of course there were no qualified staff on the ward, but somehow we coped between the three of us and got all the routine work done too. Consequently I am exhausted again, but quietly proud of the achievement too.

Gill and Henry are as dotty over each other as ever. It looks as if Gill and I will be on nights together, which is almost too good to be true and much better than playing Cox and Box in the bedroom. In no time it will be our holiday when I'm coming up to Sheffield and then on to Newcastle-under-Lyme to stay with Gill and her surrogate family (the people she lived with after her parents moved to Chelmsford so that she could complete her A levels at the same school). Part of me wants to spend the whole two weeks with you, but you'd have to work anyway, a reversal of our usual situation, so maybe this plan is better.

To bring up the subject of engagement again, I think you have misjudged me. Maybe I am jealous of friends who are already engaged, I suppose that is only natural, but I don't want to join them just to be one of the club. I want to be yours and that is different. Also it would help in fobbing off men that chat me up, like the dishy houseman with the sports car who was very persistent. I'm still wondering if he really does have black silk sheets! I do think engagement would give our lives an added extra; being able to say my fiancé instead of trying to imply the relationship in other words. Enough said. I shall continue to wait, though I'm not very good at the patiently bit! I've worked out the others are all working this weekend and we'll have lots of time alone together to talk… and just be together alone, bliss.

Letter home:

13th January 1970

I am on night duty. Not on Albert with Gill as we'd hoped, oh no. I think the office realised the two of us were on together and decided the hospital couldn't stand the efficiency. The powers that be tried to move me back to day duty when I would have had to work Sunday, but as Peter was here I risked making myself unpopular and refused. After a bit of negotiation we settled on my doing a stint of nine nights, which will be an endurance challenge but well worth it as I shall be off the weekend of Matron's Ball.

I'm supposed to be on Paget when it reopens, but there is a debate over whether to make it male or female as there is an equal demand for beds. We suggested making it mixed, but no one is taking us seriously. Meanwhile I'm in the pool and get sent to the busiest ward every night – what have I done to deserve this?

Night duty is like a set reunion: I've never seen so many third years on nights. Where have all the juniors gone? Gill and I did get one night working together which was fun, but then I got sent to Musgrave (women's surgical) with seven drips to get through on schedule, not to mention a grand total of fifty-five blood pressures to take. Then I was moved to Tipperary (men's surgical) which was equally hectic. In addition to the usual post-op checks, we had a patient who was seriously disorientated and convinced he was in his own house and we were intruders. I was delegated to try and calm him down. Chatting to him in a gentle way, I moved slowly closer as I thought I was gaining his confidence. Not a bit of it. He threw the entire contents of his full water jug over me, moving surprisingly fast for an old boy and drenching me very efficiently. Everyone else thought it hilarious, and I mean everyone as the ranting and raving had woken the whole ward. We had to get the porters up to hold him down whilst we gave him an injection to sedate him, which was sad but necessary. It was a sleepless night all round, and the patients all wanted cups of tea, which explains why there was no time to write letters then and this is rather a sleepy effort as I'm longing for bed, but I promise to write a more coherent letter soon.

Darling Peter,

I'm writing at work. Once again I am all on my own.
Paget has reopened, but only has eight patients. I quite like
being alone because I can organise things my way and don't
have to work with someone I dislike, as sometimes happens.
I enjoy my breaks twice as much because it is a joy to have
someone to talk to. Rita and Gill have finished nights now,
but Angie is keeping me company and Dawn is being super-
efficient on the ward next door.

It is easy to lose track of time and I was suddenly reminded
that this weekend is our first anniversary, and I'm not seeing
you. I should be feeling down in the dumps, but a peaceful
night on my own gives me time to think of you, and us,
the wonderful times we have had and our future together.
Why are so many of my nursing friends having problems
with their parents over their boyfriends? Why do parents
manage to make their children hostile when they are trying
to hang on to them? I consider myself lucky to have sensible,
modern, open-minded parents who help to increase my love
and happiness instead of trying to ruin it. I think we are all
a bit touchy at the moment and getting to the stage when we
need a holiday.

It definitely looks as if we shall all be going to the ball.
Everyone I speak to is going so goodness knows who is
running the hospital. It is Rag Day the first weekend of block
and we can go into town together. There will be floats again,
and as I missed the last two years it would be fun to go this
time, especially with you.

Thank you for all the happiness and joy, peace and
security, friendship and love you have given me in this last
precious year.

Oh dear! The men are waking up and demanding
bedpans, cups of tea, etc. My dreams are shattered and duty
calls once more. I must get some more sixpences on the way
home ready to phone you again.

I've been spending lots of money. I bought my sewing machine, twenty-first present from my Godmother, which I got £5 cheaper in the sales and could afford curling tongs with the money saved. The money my grandmother gave me is all going on clothes. I'm making two new skirts to enhance my wardrobe.

The Nursery seems dominated by niggles over petty things. I admit to getting pernickety about my possessions. I hate the others borrowing them without permission and not using them carefully. I've made rules that no one is to use my sewing machine unless I am here and never to borrow my curling tongs without asking first. I don't want to sound mean, but now I can afford some really nice things I would be angry and upset if they were ruined.

My record player has been mended; it needed a new valve.

Even your description of the flat can't put me off coming to Sheffield, and I guess I might even run to a bit of cooking and cleaning to help earn my keep. Yes please, it would be fantastic if you could pick Gill and me up in Newcastle and drive us back to Cambridge. Of course we will pay your petrol, lots cheaper than train fares. Longing to hear your voice on Thursday at seven o'clock and living for being with you on Friday.

Letter home:

27th January 1970

I wish I was coming home as I am so tired at present. All of us are desperately in need of holidays. Peter worries I'll be bored in Sheffield, but really it will be wonderful not to have to do anything, go anywhere, think, remember, or make decisions. I shall thoroughly enjoy lying in late and being completely idle, reading in bed (because it is the warmest place) and just about getting up in time to see Peter in his lunch hour.

Peter has given me a lovely smoked glass flower vase and a bunch of freesias to go in it to celebrate our first anniversary.

Such a thoughtful present as I buy flowers from the market nearly every week and this vase will be perfect for sweet peas in the summer.

27th January 1970

Darling Peter,

Gill and I went round to Annie's super clean house for tea yesterday. As we left she said, "Have a good holiday, see you in block." I could hardly believe it. Time is passing amazingly quickly and we seem to have achieved so much since getting our third year belts only four months ago.

Everyone looks washed out and weary, and we sleep until the alarms rudely awaken us. We are getting short-tempered at work too, although I think the juniors are partly the cause. Things are not what they used to be. We often work late whilst they consider it is their right to go off duty on time! What is nursing coming to?

Paget is a lovely little ward with a congenial atmosphere and great working conditions. At the moment we have got some grotty, miserable female patients, but the ward is still fun. I almost wish I was coming back here after block, but I doubt that will happen.

Angie failed her driving test, but is not unduly concerned. It is well known the examiners fail females first time on principle. She's put in to take it again as soon as possible.

Most of our conversations revolve around holidays, exams and weddings. It seems funny to think that when I come up to Sheffield I shall probably be exploring the town where our first home will be. I am counting the days, and even the minutes, until I am with you.

Letter home from Newcastle-under-Lyme:

10th February 1970

The holiday is flying by. I had a wonderful week in Sheffield with Peter, but not without event. The flat he shares is very bachelor and basic, take that totally literally, but rather romantic despite that. There is only a two bar electric fire for heat, no curtains, a chair which collapses if you sit in it, rain dripping through the ceiling, wallpaper coming off the damp walls and hanging in artistic strips, and electric light bulbs with no shades. Why romantic? You may well ask.

A little round table with two serviceable chairs is situated in a bow window on a slightly raised dais. The flat is on the top floor of a house which sits on top of a hill and all Sheffield is spread out in the valley. Dirty, grimy old steel works Sheffield by day, yes, but by night it becomes a wonderland of twinkling lights creating a breath-taking view and the perfect place for a candlelit supper.

Peter took me to meet his uncle in Leeds and he treated us to Sunday lunch at Monk Fryston Hall. He ordered champagne and persuaded me to try pheasant cooked in a brandy sauce, delicious!

The flat is now a lot cleaner. I had not planned to be washing the ceilings and all the walls, but I was the one that set the chip pan on fire. Stupidly I thought I'd indulge Peter with chips for lunch and used their pan full of lard which ignited from the gas flame. Despite me moving amazingly quickly to extinguish the gas and cover the pan with a damp towel (thank God for all that time learning such things at Guides), the kitchen, hall and part of the sitting room were transformed into the black hole of Calcutta. Fortunately Peter was so relieved it was not any worse and I wasn't hurt, well only my ego, he helped that evening with the scrubbing and so did his flatmates. It turned into quite a jolly joint cleaning effort. I bought the beer, and the flat is now more hygienic. As the landlord never visits he will never know. Funny way to spend a holiday; lucky Peter still loves me!

We nearly got stranded in the snow on the Snake Pass as well; it's been a crazy week.

Darling Peter,

Gill and I are sharing a double bed; believe me I'd rather share one with you! Parting after our week together felt very hard and the train journey was a nightmare. Now I'm here we are having a good time and it's a joy to relax and have someone else cooking all the meals. We put on our best Cambridge University accents to visit Gill's posh friend. She picked us up in her Capri, no less, and we even got a demonstration of the much famed electric bread knife – whatever next? Gill cleaned The Nursery before she left, bless her, and says the landlady has had the storage heater fixed, hoorah. It will be both spick and span and cosy when we return at the weekend.

I do miss you.

18th February 1970

Back to work with a crunch. Blue Block has highlighted how much anatomy and physiology has slipped my mind and it feels very odd to be back in the school room. Another phase of the New Site has opened and the School of Nursing has officially moved up here. The whole place is desperately overheated and airless, and that gave me a splitting headache. We have late lectures until 5.30pm every day, and a break of one and a half hours at lunchtime which is infuriating: too short to get anywhere and back again, and too long to be idling the time away. Such is life. On the plus side I am mostly enjoying using my brain again, and some of the consultants' lectures are very interesting.

One of the tutors is a pain and I crossed swords with her today. I'm tired of being expected to run a ward one minute and being treated like a schoolgirl the next. Added to all this I am on the change list to go to Ward 2 after Blue Block which I'm not that happy about, too many unconscious patients. I shall request nights straight away in the hopes of getting Easter off.

I've finished the jumper for my sister's birthday present and I've taught myself to crochet to use up all the odd balls of wool, making a huge multicoloured bedspread. Life at The Nursery is none too good, friction all round. I can't explain why, but we seem to be getting on each other's nerves, which is sad as we were all looking forward to this time together. Gill and I are fine, but she goes out every evening to be with Henry. It is impossible to work in the lounge with Angie, Rita and Liz wittering on, and I have taken to coming to bed early with a hot water bottle to study and then read. That ensures I don't open my big mouth and say something we might all regret, but I shall probably be accused of not speaking to them instead.

The winter aconites are out on the backs and I've seen two crocus flowers, promising spring will soon be here. Every weekend seems to be someone's twenty-first birthday party, which will be tiring but good fun. The Eightsome's party is this Friday at the University Air Squadron, which I'm looking forward to as they are such good friends. You'll enjoy seeing Steve and Ros again. It seems ages since we were with them at the May Ball.

22nd February 1970

I just had to tell someone the news, and it has to be you because I promised you I would not tell anyone else! The most wonderful thing is going to happen at Easter and the very thought of it makes my spirits soar. I love you so very, very much and I am ecstatic that we will be declaring this to the world. The weekend was wonderful, quiet and peaceful, snuggly and cuddly and perfectly lovely. I have been unbelievably careful not to show the slightest sign of being abnormally happy, but I'm certain Angie has guessed. She keeps mentioning Easter and giving me knowing looks which I am careful to ignore.

The classroom was a comedown after a fabulous weekend with you, but lectures today held my interest, which was a miracle when I have a head full of thoughts about our future together. This comes from the girl you are making the happiest in the world. I hug our secret, think of you and see the world through rose coloured spectacles. I will love you beyond eternity.

25th February 1970

Gill was looking longingly at engagement rings today and likes the £12 one in the antique shop by Great St Mary's Church that we admired, but then she spotted a very similar, and I think nicer, one for 12 guineas in the jewellers next to WHSmith. It would definitely suit her thin fingers better than my square hand, and she saw it first so I shall have to continue looking for the perfect one for us.

I've got a horrible, stuffy, sneezy cold (perhaps it is as well these kisses come by post) and the central heating at the New Site is not helping. Gill was worse than me with stomach pains, diarrhoea and vomiting. She had to make a quick exit from the lecture, and I made my escape to look after her. We missed a boring lecture; Gill bought a box of coffee chocolates to say thank you and we are having a secret bedtime guzzle as it wouldn't be fair on Angie's diet to eat them in front of her.

The weather is lovely, just like spring, if rather cold. There are lots of snowdrops out in the gardens on the way into town. I couldn't help but think optimistically it means Easter is nearly here.

2nd March 1970

It is March already, but freezing cold and it has snowed!

I couldn't get to sleep last night. I was missing your warm body beside me, then I got cramp and then, just as I was drifting off, I started to cough, cough, cough and had to dive under the covers to muffle the noise, trying not to disturb Gill. I've been sleepy all day, and the lecture on Ideology wasn't exactly stimulating. Pay day tomorrow means I can afford to go into town on my afternoon off and get the wool for the jumper I plan to knit for Father's birthday. I shall look at material for a new dress too as I need to look my best for you at Easter!

It has been snowing heavily all day and our spirits have been decidedly lowered. I'm sure the tutors couldn't understand our focus on the white skies and the depth of snow on the ground. At last it is thawing and the roads are beautifully slushy. We got soaked by passing cars as we cycled home, but we don't care because it feels much warmer and the roads should be clear by the weekend allowing our beloved men to come.

Gill and I bought two dress patterns to share, but I decided not to get any material yet because I'm meant to be studying. Life at The Nursery continues to be problematic as we are all on top of each other and the house seems much smaller. There is lots of friction and frayed nerves, especially with an important exam looming.

Tell your computer from me that if it isn't nice to your discs I shall be very cross with it and never come to visit. Don't work so hard that you are exhausted at the weekend. Thank you for apologising, but, honestly, there was no need. I know you are worried about your mother's reaction to us getting engaged, but remember I shall be beside you supporting you and it will be the two of us united to face any, and all, problems throughout the rest of our lives. Now I shall close my eyes, snuggle down in bed and dream of being close to you.

I didn't write until today as I've been trying to get my off duty. Sadly I have got to work a B shift on Sunday, so it would be sensible if you drove back to Sheffield then. The good news is I'm down to go on nights and will finish

Maundy Thursday morning and be off duty until Easter Tuesday, which is perfect.

I'm feeling much better this week after tender loving care from both you and Mother at the weekend. I hope things were better between your parents when you phoned them. I know the continual problems worry you. This morning we had a late start so I had a lovely, long, luxurious sleep and woke up smiling, and the grin got wider when I heard I had got Easter off, hoorah! I must get on with some studying. Though I long for Friday, there is work to be completed afore then.

On 14th March Peter bought the engagement ring. I had found two contenders, fortunately in the same antique shop: one a sapphire and the other an emerald. He had the final say. As the ring had to be enlarged, we arranged that I would collect it the next week and then went to The Green Man for a drink to celebrate. We were very lucky as the day after I collected it the jeweller's shop was broken into and all the remaining rings were stolen.

17th March 1970

Ward 2. After all that time sitting in lectures I'm not used to the heavy workload and rushing around all day; my shoulders ache and my legs are killing me. When I got back last night I did my washing, wrote some letters, had a bath, and collapsed into bed exhausted and slept like the dead.

I spent yesterday and today in The Annexe: that is the section for the intensive care patients. It is blissful compared to the main ward because I can get things more organised, and you know I prefer being my own boss. The little girl in here has captured my heart and it is exciting because she is inching slowly towards getting better. She was knocked down by a car and has been unconscious for ages and nursed in a freezing cold room to lower her body's demands and give her time to heal. Every day her mother sits beside her, reading aloud from her favourite alphabet book called Ant and Bee. When the doctors decided to warm her body, she eventually stirred and woke up. Her first words were Ant and Bee! It was an emotional moment and proves to me, beyond doubt, that unconscious people can hear.

I hope to see a great improvement in her during my time on this ward. She might even be walking again before I leave as children improve much quicker than adults. There's a super crowd going on night duty which will make the time go faster. Easter is nearly here, you had better start practising going down on one knee!

19th March 1970

Mother came over yesterday for my day off. I don't know how I kept a straight face when she said, "Are you two ever going to bother getting engaged?"

I answered, "Oh yes, probably" very calmly in an off-hand way and nearly burst trying not to say anything else.

I'm afraid I have a confession to make: Angie knows about the ring. I thought I had fielded all her enquiries successfully, but she is a very intuitive person. She has an incredible knack of quite naturally and unconsciously catching one unawares and guessing the truth. I've sworn her to secrecy, and actually it will be quite useful as she's going to help cover up the fact I'm going to collect it Monday morning. I'm sorry, Darling, but she caught me off guard. Ironic isn't it? I said if anyone found out it would be Angie, but our secret is safe with her.

I think Mother will be truly pleased about our engagement. She accepts it is as good as done anyway, but I can feel she is dying to talk weddings. You know what we women are like. We both find it frustrating having nothing to do with the plans for Liz and Paul's wedding, except to hope they have a plan as they still have not fixed the date.

I cut my new dress out yesterday and hope to get the machining finished tonight. Everything is going to be wonderful despite the depletion of your bank balance.

You should think of it as an investment that will show tremendous profits, maybe not financial ones, but certainly priceless ones.

Letter home:

This is the first time I've sat down tonight and it is 3am. We expected it to be quiet, but lots of niggling little things keep happening to keep us on the trot.

Peter and I will come home Maundy Thursday afternoon and stay until Easter Monday, but will go and see his parents on Good Friday until the Saturday morning, assuming that is all right with you.

All five of us are on nights and it feels strange all of us going to bed together in the mornings and getting up in the evening. We are used to it being one or two of us, but the whole house living upside down is bizarre.

I still don't know when the exam results will be out and am starting to get fidgety waiting. Also the dress I am making at the moment is proving rather fiddly and taking longer than anticipated, but I still hope to get it finished to wear at Easter.

24th March 1970

Darling Peter,

Once again a quiet night. It is 3.30am, and apart from observations, turns and feeds every one to two hours I have little to do. Sometimes we wonder what we are doing up at this unearthly hour as we would much rather be busy and feel useful, but when I think of my nights off it all seems worthwhile.

I've just checked the off duty rota. I come back to work on Easter Tuesday and am down for nights again on the Thursday. If all my nights are as quiet as these I shall get loads of knitting done. Annie popped in during her break for a chat. She's so upbeat she livens us all up, and she worked out that my next lot of nights off are over her twenty-first party so we'll be able to go. Hoorah, something else for us to look forward to.

Later in the night a funny thing happened. I had gone up to borrow something from the orthopaedic ward, and as I was walking down the corridor to the nurses' station I heard a patient call out, "Nurse, nurse!" I recognised that voice immediately, and I was right: it was a patient I had nursed at Chesterton. She was 103 then, and is 104 now. This time she has a fractured shaft of femur so I doubt she'll make 105, but she is such a determined lady you never know.

I'm longing for Thursday. I'll only need to sleep for about three hours to set me up and I'm hoping you'll arrive as soon as possible after that. I'm trying not to peep at the ring, but it is too tempting. It is absolutely beautiful, both for itself and even more so for what it will represent before very long. I admit I am excited, but deep down inside there is a steady certainty of our love and I know this is simply a small step in our life together.

On Maundy Thursday I had a few hours' sleep after night duty, and was up, dressed and alone in the house when Peter arrived at The Nursery. As I went to the kitchen to put the kettle on, I casually mentioned, "By the way, the ring is in the box on the mantelpiece."

When I returned to the lounge, Peter went down on one knee and asked me to marry him. I said, "Of course I will", and at 2.45pm (I noted the time that night in my diary) we became engaged. It wasn't a particularly romantic setting, but it was definitely the most wonderful moment. The air was alive with the intensity of our feelings and love filled the ordinary room. I pulled Peter off his knees and fell into his arms. Nothing else mattered. No one could have been happier.

Letter home:

4th April 1970

Despite an early night I am still feeling tired, but what matter. It was a wonderful Easter and you fed us so well I've put on half a stone. Thank you.

Peter is glad you all approve of him as my fiancé. I can't get used to that word, it still sounds strange.

Exam results came out yesterday. I came third, 63 per cent, which amazed me and just goes to show the overall standard was pretty low. Apparently eight failed out of the thirty, including Liz, again. She doesn't seem to be thinking clearly about what she is going to do, which is strange because at work she is very decisive. It's a relief to know that it is a clear road to finals now.

I had expected to be on the change list (for a new ward) but my name is not there, which means I shall have to go to the office and make enquiries. The best thing about working shifts is I hardly miss Peter at the weekend because it is hard to remember when the weekend is.

5th April 1970

Darling Peter,

Thank you for your letter which cheered me up considerably because I was three quarters of an hour late off duty and a bit fed up.

Good news, I've managed to get next weekend's off duty changed in our favour. I have Friday evening off and only have to work Saturday morning, and will either be off on Sunday or on night duty again. Either way I can spend all day with you.

Everyone sends their congratulations on our engagement. The hospital grapevine seems to have gone into overdrive with the most unexpected people congratulating me – or should I say us? It is wonderful that people are happy for us. When Angie asked me whether I thought engagement had made much difference – trust her to ask a thought provoking question – I had to stop and think. I suppose the answer is both yes and no. Certainly it has made both of us spectacularly happy and it does offer a kind of comfort in the loneliness of our days spent away from each other. Also it makes marriage seem closer, which is very special. I am pleased and relieved that your mother seemed to accept us. She shows so little emotion it is difficult to know for sure, but I felt it all went smoothly, which bodes well for the future.

How's life at The Nursery? Angie is miserable. Liz is upset about her exam results and still doesn't seem to have any plans. Rita is full of the joys because spring is here. Gill is frustrated as once again her future in-laws do not approve of them getting married until Henry is fully qualified. I do feel sorry for them as that must feel like, and is, ages away.

My threepenny bit collection is full and I must count it up and bank it soon, then we can spend it. You must have lots and lots of Green Shield Stamps by now with all the petrol you buy. I really ought to get on with a thousand and one jobs, but first I must tell you that a beautiful sapphire is twinkling on my finger and telling the whole world how much in love we are. Did I explain that at work we are not allowed to wear rings in case we scratch the patients? Instead it hangs from a safety pin on my breast pocket so it is always with me and close to my heart.

7th April 1970

Day off today. Angie's sleeping, all the others are working and I'm on my own. I must go into town to buy some new black shoes because I had to stitch one of this pair back together this morning. I'll pop into the hospital, see the Assistant Matron and try to get the rest of my training sorted out. I do like to know where I stand and hate the uncertainty over the amount of sick leave I had to have at the beginning and whether or not that will affect finals. I'll attempt to get my exam paper back too just to see where I did get all those marks.

What news is there? Well I'm overworked, underpaid and madly in love, which I guess you already knew. Sister did me the great honour yesterday of saying, "I want you to be acting staff nurse this morning." In plain English that means "You can run the ward and do all the work whilst I chat to the doctors." Actually it was satisfying to be able to organise things and consequently get everything done efficiently and all of us off duty on time.

Liz is keeping a big secret: her wedding date and plans for the future. We are all worried she will chuck nursing in, which would be very, very silly at this stage of training. More importantly, she's a damn good nurse. If only she could pass exams! I wish I knew how best to help her.

I actually did some gardening yesterday. I clipped back the Virginia creeper to stop it climbing through the kitchen and dining room windows. Now you can see how dirty the windows are and someone ought to clean them and polish the lounge floor as it hasn't been done since I last did it five months ago. I expect you can guess who 'someone' is? Why do these things irritate me before the others even notice them? Now I'm looking out of the window and it has started snowing, in April!

14th April 1970

Great news, stop press, written as I heard it: Angie has passed her driving test. Heaven help us all!

After you left early yesterday I went back to bed and slept blissfully until 10.30am. Just as well as all hell was let loose on Ward 2, and the annexe was in chaos when I got there for the afternoon shift. There were two big theatre cases, as if one isn't enough to cope with, and then into the bargain a chap arrived from Accident Service. A girder fell from a crane onto his head, quite messy really, and I hadn't even got a bed to put the poor man into as no one had informed us he was coming. No sooner had I got him sorted out than one patient arrived back from theatre and the other had to go. It was ridiculous as I only had one junior (who had never done neuro before) to help me. I'm glad to say everything was just about shipshape when it was time to hand over and go off duty, but I was exhausted, both mentally and physically.

This morning was somewhat better as everything was under control, but, of course, I was on my own with three seriously ill patients and one other to look after, and consequently was rushed off my feet. I never got my coffee break, but to be honest I never noticed. I'm not complaining as it was all very interesting and the time flew by. I prefer it that way and, even better, all the patients are improving.

Liz and I had a big heart to heart. She poured all her troubles out, tears and all. She's much more cheerful now and I think she realises she can't please everybody all the time. Sometimes she seems to have an almost pathological need to keep everyone happy, and not being able to achieve that makes her the unhappy one. I hope talking helped her, and I know it has helped me appreciate how she is feeling. I didn't give any advice, I simply listened and asked occasional questions. It is surprising how helpful that seems to be. I'm glad she is back to her usual sunny self.

20th April 1970

We had a very quiet night on the ward and I attempted the skeleton crossword, but failed miserably without your assistance. I finished knitting the front of Father's jumper, which was more productive. By the way, our threepenny bits added up to £4:8s:0d.

I'm sitting in the dining room and the sun is streaming in on my back making me feel warm and cosy and very, very sleepy. It is nearly nine o'clock so I shall say good-night and make Gill a cuppa to wake her up in a civilised way as I go to bed. A tired night nurse in Cambridge is quite wonderfully in love with you and still basking in the glow of a perfect weekend.

22nd April 1970

No letter for me, four for Gill and one each for Liz and Angie. I assume you are busy, or the GPO is up to its usual tricks.

The nights seem to be going very slowly. The patients are a miserable bunch of 'feel sorry for themselves' types. I suppose that is not their fault, but it does dampen my spirits, making it harder to appear always cheerful on duty, and I am decidedly lethargic. I feel as if I am in a state of suspended animation. You know that feeling that you are doing everything automatically and nothing really touches you. I suppose it is a defence mechanism because one of the cases I am nursing at the moment is heartbreaking: a middle aged lady who had come in as an urgent case to have an aneurysm on a blood vessel in her brain repaired. Sadly, when she was all prepped and ready to go to theatre, it burst. The doctors worked hard to stabilise her condition, but the brain damage from the haemorrhage is too great now for surgery.

Friends comment on how quiet I am because it is so unlike me. I shut myself into a little world of thoughts of you and our future and only seem to emerge when Gill or Angie is around as they have a way of making me feel more myself without so much as a comment. I'm not miserable, but I am looking forward to nights off and a bit of TLC from Mother. Six weeks on Ward 2 is long enough, and this last bit is rather a strain.

Continued:

24th April 1970

It is a beautiful morning with the sun streaming through the trees, shining on the blossom and daffodils and making the dew glisten on the cobwebs. I'm feeling happy and peaceful. My little lady died in the early hours. At the time it was an ordeal with relatives to console, but once it was all over and I'd delivered her safely to the mortuary I felt much lighter.

At the usual time, seven o'clock this morning, the ward telephone rang. I stared at it in disbelief, for why would her husband be phoning to enquire how she was when he had been with her when she died? I took a deep breath and picked the receiver up, and a voice said, "It did really happen, didn't it, nurse?" and I knew then how very true it is that people never die for those that love them. Even death cannot part two people who have a deep, close and loving relationship.

He accepted her death wonderfully well and was very sweet, saying his thanks to us all. I think he just needed someone to talk to. I feel as if I should be thanking him for showing me the extent and power of human love. I had always thought it was so, but now I know for certain. No wonder it is such a beautiful morning.

I can hear Angie making 'awake' noises and I'm supposed to be going up with a cup of tea and her twenty-first present as I shan't see her on her birthday tomorrow. I must do that.

27th April 1970

It was wonderful talking to you on the phone tonight. It's silly of me I know, but I was missing you so terribly much, probably made worse because I was overtired. I knew you had not written because you are overworked at the moment, but the lack of concrete communication with you for so long a period, coupled with the fact that I'd had a terrible week, all got a bit much. I'm not upset or annoyed with you at all, it is just that our enforced separation, overtiredness and emotional strain united, and the moment I heard your voice I burst into tears then couldn't really explain why. I'll try to now.

Night duty, which usually comes as a welcome respite from days, was very stressful this time. Because I was worried I slept badly, and then things seemed even worse. This built up steadily until my little lady died. I only told you one side of the story; the responsibility of it all is another tale. Staff Nurse had opted out, forcing me into what should have been her role. Convincing myself that this was good experience, that she trusted me and anyway I shall soon be a staff nurse myself, I decided I could cope with the situation...which I did. The doctor had been in to confirm the death, but then left and it fell to me to switch off the ventilator in front of all the relatives at the bedside. It was a horrid moment because it looked as if I was stopping the breathing and killing the patient, even though I and the relatives knew her heart had stopped a while ago.

At the time I was alright, and I think I handled the situation in a caring and professional way. As I told you the relief afterwards was incredible, and when I was cycling home I was happy and full of the beauty of nature. I slept the sleep of the exhausted that day, and if I had not had to go back on duty that night I would probably have been fine. Faced with the annexe again and more seriously ill patients I'm afraid the stress compounded.

Death evokes lots of emotions and new thoughts. I'd experienced two within five nights, and had the prospect of a third facing me. I have to show a capable, efficient nurse exterior, but I am often deeply affected. Although it is my fortune to be able to give sympathy, strength and comfort to others, it is at those times that I most need it myself. Of course I coped with that last night, and the third death, professionally, as one does. Angie and Gill did their best to support me, and Mother was, as always, wonderful, but none of that meant as much to me as hearing your voice. Your final 'I love you', inexplicable and strange as it may seem, turned the tap back on, opening the floodgates of weary relief, and I came to bed and sobbed and sobbed as I have not cried for years. Now I'm ready to face the world again.

By the way, Mother and Father are collecting threepenny bits for us, isn't that sweet of them? Also my old school has asked me to go back and chat to any girls contemplating going into the medical professions to explain what they are letting themselves in for. Do they really want, or need, to hear the whole truth?

It's now well after midnight and I must sleep. I feel happy and warm and close to you. I expect you are in bed too and thinking of me, so in that sense we are together all through the night. Don't worry about me. I'll be OK.

5th May 1970

It's another gloriously sunny day, but I only get to enjoy it cycling to and from work. It takes it out of me working in

144

these uniforms in this heat, especially when I think that this time last year I was lazing around at Fulbourn. Makes me wish I was back there again.

Rita went for petrol and cut the lawns yesterday. As always the sunshine has made her completely euphoric and I came in to find her dancing around in her long dress, wondering what to wear in the neckline and how to do her hair. Her twenty-first party isn't for three weeks yet!

I must finish cleaning our bedroom. I made a mammoth effort yesterday and removed piles of dust from under the beds. If I don't do some washing I shall have no clean undies left to wear, and it's my turn to clean the bathroom and loo. I feel exhausted just mentioning it all. I really must attack the dirt, but not until I have told you that I shall love you for ever and ever.

7th May 1970

Guess what – I've got the most perfect off duty next week. In fact I was in such raptures that I never noticed I only have one half day instead of two until Angie pointed it out. On Sunday we will have all day together, hoorah.

All hell was let loose in The Annexe again. Beautifully hot sunny weather it may be outside, but in there it is ****** freezing! Sister even let us keep our cardigans on! Three patients are having hypothermia treatment, with one in the cooling room and another on the hypothermia machine; that leaves ice packs and ice soaked towels on the third. To complicate matters further two of them are being put on respirators. Typical that I shall be leaving just as it all starts getting interesting. I actually enjoyed the shift this morning for the first time in weeks.

I hope this fabulous weather continues over the weekend as it would be wonderfully relaxing, especially being with you.

18th May 1970

The sun has been blazing all day and it is very hot. I didn't wake up until 11.30am, but then I leapt up, remarkably quickly for me, and set about 1,001 jobs. I stripped Gill's and my beds and remade them, put the washing machine on and then had to mop the kitchen as the waste pipe wasn't in the sink and I walked back in to find the floor was awash. Also I had to relight the boiler because Liz had left the ash door open last night by mistake and it had gone out. After all that I thought I deserved a rest and indulged in a delicious cup of coffee with the leftover cream floating on top and ate bananas on toast, my favourite breakfast.

Renewed in strength and vigour I hung the washing out to dry and cleaned the bathroom and downstairs loo, including the insides of the cupboards and polishing the loo seats. Then I popped to the shops to get Gill's, Angie's and the house shopping. I was going to phone Singer about my sewing machine, but the queue outside the phone box was three deep so I decided that could wait until tomorrow. Back at the house I had another cuppa and finished knitting the sleeve of Father's jumper. Then I did the ironing.

I had just finished all this when Gill arrived back with her mother and aunt. They'd bought a three course meal for all of us to share, which made me realise I had eaten very little all day. I was ravenous and really appreciated their thoughtfulness. Once they had gone and we'd tackled the mountain of washing up I was feeling positively worn out again – so much for a day off. Nevertheless I sat down and wrote a charming letter to the Rector, the one who came to my twenty-first party but has recently retired, to ask if he will come back to marry us. It took lots of brainpower, crossings out and rewriting in my best handwriting with my fountain pen, but now it is ready to post. Time for bed again and dreams of you.

Letter home:

19th May 1970

There's a strong possibility I will go on nights again this coming Sunday, so plans may have to be altered.

Peter enjoyed his holiday here even though the sun only

came out whilst I was on duty. Friday evening he took me to The Chequers at Eynesbury, as he promised ages ago, and it is the most fantastic restaurant I have ever been to. They even asked us if we had eaten enough or would we like some more? We came out after three courses, two cups of coffee each, half a bottle of Hock and a complimentary carnation for me for a fiver. We ate solidly for two hours, the service was excellent and we weren't rushed at all, the food was delicious, and my goodness, you should have seen the size of the helpings. I was so full I had difficulty eating my way through quite the largest meringue I have ever seen in my life. Peter says he thinks you and Father should take us there sometime soon. I think you'd be very impressed.

Guess what, the Socratic Society meeting I missed on Wednesday (duty called) was Mountbatten speaking and HRH Charles was there too, curses.

26th May 1970

Darling Peter,

My sister is staying and it is fun to have her company. I arrived home to the sound of her typewriter. Mother had delivered her with mountains of food so you might think I'd be putting on weight, but not at all, although I am eating like a horse. I'm frantically knitting Father's jumper and generally being very domesticated.

By the way, a girl in our set was brave enough to go to the Family Planning Clinic only to get a flea in her ear and told to come back when she has a wedding ring on her finger. She told them she is trying to be sensible, but all to no avail. She was firmly shown the door. This means all the rest of us will need to find another source of the pill or go on waiting. Perhaps being engaged will make a difference.

28th May 1970

The Singer sewing machine man failed to turn up despite my waiting to the last possible minute and then dashing to the hospital to get my pay. I couldn't get it as the finance office had decided to stop paying out at one o'clock instead of half past as they always have in the past. This made me very annoyed and upset and completely scuppered my shopping plans. I went to tell the Assistant Matron exactly what I thought about it. She was very sweet and rather took the wind out of my sails by offering to lend me some cash until tomorrow. I said I was only inconvenienced. It was the principle I wanted to get across that we could have been warned of the time change. She smiled and said I'd made my point in no uncertain terms and we parted amicably. I walked on into town to remonstrate with Singer, but, would you believe it, they were shut for half day closing.

This evening we saw Kes at the Vic which we thought was beautifully filmed, especially the shots of the kestrel. Arriving back at the house, I discovered I had left my keys inside in my empty purse as I'm living off my rich little sister at the moment. For once the downstairs was well and truly locked up, but Sis did a grand job of climbing onto the garage roof and in through Liz's bedroom window.

Seeing all the May Ball posters and the degree photos and gowns in the shop windows in town makes last year a poignant memory and I wish you were back here again and we could relive that wonderful end of term. On the other hand I am glad it is now and I am a year nearer to marrying my darling clever Wrangler, whom I love a million times more for knowing you better, always and forever.

31st May 1970

It was lovely hearing you on the phone tonight, the first time in ages you have phoned me on night duty. It cheers me up no end.

We've had some hilarious nights. Gill is on too (in the Blue Room, intensive care) and she told this black-as-night African houseman to come and see us on Musgrave (women's surgical) for some scrambled eggs. Honestly when he walked down the ward all I could see was his white coat and smiling teeth approaching. He is great fun, and so is this group of patients. One woman is incredibly crude and yet very amusing with it, and has us all in hysterics, including Night Sister.

Tonight the ward is uncannily quiet and I'm having difficulty staying awake despite frequent cups of coffee. It is 3.45am and already it is starting to get light outside...Pause for half a dozen bedpans...Now the birds are singing and here comes Gill to eat our chocolates as they don't seem to get given any in the Blue Room.

Gill and Henry are having a party on Thursday evening, so I shall pop in before coming on nights as Henry's friends are a good crowd and it will be fun, even if it makes me miss you horribly. I shall have to finish now as it is time to write up the Kardex, a flip card record of all the patients, and the report for Night Sister, and get organised for the morning rush.

2nd June 1970

Night duty continues in the never ceasing round of working hard and sleeping soundly. Gill being on nights at the same time helps keep us both sane and laughing. The patients are all moans and groans tonight and two of them are completely round the twist. It's three o'clock already and this is my first break. The ward was chaotic when I came on and it took ages to get everything finished. Why are some people incapable of getting their share of the work done, and done properly? I still have loads to do, but I'll get it all finished somehow or other, even if I'm late off.

It's starting to get light now and soon dawn will break. One advantage of nights on Musgrave is being able to go out onto the roof and watch the sun come up over the pinnacles of King's College Chapel, or look the other way and watch the sky changing colour, illuminating the spire of the Catholic Church. I shan't have time for that tonight, but believe me it is incredibly beautiful, peaceful and most romantic. When I'm there I wish you could be with me instead of only in my thoughts.

At this point my musing was abruptly shattered. One of our mad ladies decided to leap out of bed and make a dash for the door with drip, drain and catheter in tow. From then on there was no peace, and no breaks, until now when I'm back at the house feeling shattered and ready for bed. Gill's come in – bedtime.

8th June 1970

I'm writing this from my parents' house, and Mother's planned a big birthday celebration for Father and Sis. It is definitely not jumper weather, but at least it fits and he likes it. It is too hot for comfort, but I went to the dentist and shopping before I collapsed on the lawn this afternoon and went back to sleep.

Continued:

Mother and I went to London. We fought our way through the stores getting hot and frustrated. I managed to buy a pair of sandals and then we went to Mappin and Webb – talk about posh, it was beautiful. I was choosing my twenty-first present from my parents and I saw the most gorgeous coffee pot, but it was £193, sadly much too expensive. I looked more carefully, and after due consideration I settled on a set of six solid silver grapefruit spoons which I'm delighted with.

Tomorrow morning I'm following Mother's advice and placing my body at the mercy of an osteopath. I feel awfully nervous, but hope he can cure this constant nagging backache. It's been bad ever since I moved an unconscious patient by myself on Ward 2, my own silly fault I know, but there was no one to help and it had to be done. Think of me.

22nd June 1970

We had such a fantastic time last night. We went to Great St Mary's Church for Evensong as Cliff Richard was making a guest appearance. Despite us getting there early, the place was packed, and because there were no more seats we got shown to the front and sat on the floor under the pulpit which was brilliant, such a stroke of luck. He spoke very sincerely about his Christian faith and, of course, sang. It was a fabulous evening and we cycled home with soaring spirits.

30th June 1970

Horrid, horrible bad news! I've had a letter telling me I can't take finals with the rest of the set because of all the time I had off sick with Glandular Fever, just what I feared. Apparently I took one day too long. I can hardly believe it, feel really angry and shall fight it all the way. What about all the unpaid overtime I've done?

Tonight seems to be passing very slowly. I've done hardly anything except drink coffee and chat. I seem to have taken ages to complete a very small amount of written work. It is extraordinarily cold and Griffith Ward (men's medical) seems to be full of dying patients. I suppose these are the ones I see most because the better patients sleep and don't require attention. I'm glad to do what I can to keep them comfortable, but it is rather depressing.

Never mind, it is pay day tomorrow which always cheers a nurse up. I had a long chat with Night Sister tonight, the one I'm always talking about whom I've liked and admired ever since she came to my rescue on Children's Ward. She's leaving tomorrow, which is very sad because we shall all miss her help and enthusiasm. As it was quiet she suggested we had a cuppa and a chat in the office and left the middle in charge. I felt a bit embarrassed that she'd singled me out when she has all the nurses in the hospital to choose from, but we had a lovely long talk and agreed that we could do with a bit more humanity in the management. Connected to that she was very encouraging and supported my efforts to challenge the decision on my finals.

"Give it a jolly good try," she said, which felt like a vote of confidence in my abilities.

…Interruption by innumerable old men in dirty beds… all clean now…

My visit to the office was useless. All she did was to write 'Finals? Children's Ward?' on her memo pad. I don't think she listened to a word I said, but at least she didn't say I can't take finals with the others so maybe there is hope yet. It is desperately unsettling and I shall be glad when this issue is resolved. It matters so much to me; the force of my feelings is ferocious. I know my work is up to standard and I am as experienced and confident in my abilities as the rest of the set. I feel undervalued and angry. How can one measly little day too many over a period of three years make such a difference?

2nd July 1970

I'm sorry about the phone call. You really did choose the wrong moment. I had Night Sister and four doctors standing around the desk and I was away down the ward fetching some notes. Thank goodness the middle answered the phone and came to warn me it was you. Well done you for guessing the situation straight away. I longed to say, "I love you", but it had to be simply hello and goodbye with a big hint in the middle that the tests are tomorrow morning in the hopes they thought I was talking to an enquiring relative.

It worries me that one person has the power to make or break my future and it all seems so unfair. Everyone in the hospital seems to have heard and they stop and wish me good luck or say how disgustingly petty it all is. They are very kind, but it will be of little comfort if it all goes wrong.

The ward has been frantically busy the last two nights with hardly the chance of a break. We got absolutely no thanks from Sister in the morning despite the fact we got twice as much done to be ready for the doctor's exams. Oh dear, I do sound crotchety, must be bedtime. What with me worried about finals and you worrying about your parents we make a right pair.

Written from my parent's house:

I feel guilty that I talked you into coming down last weekend because to me every minute of your company is worthwhile and wonderful. I now see it was selfish of me. You have to drive hundreds of miles and then often I am on duty and not here. Also I am still wound up over this finals business so it was hardly surprising you got ratty. Sometimes I get frightened and worried and feel helpless as I know you need my support, especially whilst you are worried about your father's depression and your mother's mental health. I seem to have used up all my sympathy and caring on the wards. Sorry.

I've just got back from an afternoon at my old school. What a farce, there was no one interested in nursing, though I did speak to one girl thinking of dentistry. None of my old friends were there, but I suppose I did my bit by turning up. It made me realise how little I have in common with the other girls who went on to university or college. I would never swap my life for theirs: they are pathetically immature, they don't have jobs, are still dependent on their parents and mostly don't seem to know what they want in life. I was the only one wearing a ring and I feel very lucky in every way.

Hoorah, Liz is full of wedding plans, but I think she feels her twin sister is rather stealing her thunder by suddenly getting married first. Bit of a cheeky move, poor Liz. I guess being one of twins is a tricky thing.

21st July 1970

I'm glad it is my day off tomorrow. Griffith is heavy work at present. Sister has been giving me a touch of the 'senior' treatment though, which does great things for my ego. I worked an A shift today instead of my half day so that I can have a half day on Saturday when you are here, Sunday off and a B on Monday. We'll have lots of time together. Originally I was on the rota to go on nights Tuesday to Tuesday and

I wouldn't have been able to see you for two weekends. I played the sob story, the right to occasional decent off duty, went down on my knees and pleaded and finally got today's shift changed so we can have one reasonable weekend. A minor miracle!

I must drop your parents a line and thank them for the chocolates. I think Bendick's Bittermints will always be my favourites. Hope your mother is improving again and then your father will feel better too.

I've bought the tickets for us to see The Seagull. The cheapest left were 12s and I got the last two seats together.

Gill arrived back after a wonderful time in Newcastle. The vicar announced their engagement from the pulpit during the church service and wished them every happiness. Poor Gill and Henry nearly died from embarrassment with all the well meaning parishioners congratulating them. Secretly I think they loved it. Needless to say she and I have opposite duties the rest of the week and then she goes on nights the week after me. C'est la vie.

Talk in the dining room has veered from work to weddings as the set above start to leave and their friends drive to the ends of England to watch many a happy occasion and return to tell the rest of us all the details. Their finals results come out next Monday which should change the conversation. I bet the most overworked phrase will be 'us next'. Thank God that now includes me!

Why? What suddenly caused the powers that be to change their minds?

"Oh, Nurse Walker, this is for you."

The news came unexpectedly, written on a folded sheet of paper handed to me by the ward clerk. I read the typed statement:

Nurse Walker, your name has been added to the list of student nurses who will sit final examinations at the next session.

Was this really true or some kind of sick practical joke? The notepaper had no official heading, nor was the message signed. Could I believe it? The ward was busy and I worked on automatic pilot whilst my brain was occupied pondering this possibility. My hopes were soaring despite a nasty niggling fear that it would prove to be a cruel mistake. As soon as Sister said we could take a coffee break, I whipped my apron off and legged it down the flight of stairs and along the corridor, walking as fast as I dared to the official notice board. My eyes zoomed to the bottom of the alphabetical list and there it was: Eileen Walker, my name in black and white. For a minute I stared at it, close to tears. Then the smile started and I rushed to the dining room to find a friend, bursting to share the news. Everyone, like me, wanted to know why? What had caused the unpredictable change of heart? Had my good ward reports swung things in my favour, or maybe my favourite Night Sister had put in a word in support of me and influenced the decision, who knows? I decided it was best to leave well alone, be grateful, keep quiet and not ask questions. It was an indescribable relief and made me ecstatically happy.

30th July 1970

What a lovely morning: pay day and a letter from you as well.

The ward is still full of old men, but I am getting quite fond of some of them. They seem more vulnerable during the night. I often wonder why people are much friendlier at night, and think if everybody was as nice during the daytime the hospital would be a better place altogether.

I had a strange experience tonight. When the ward had settled down and the patients were asleep, we were sitting around the desk doing paperwork, and as senior I thought I ought to be friendly to the new nursing auxiliary and started a whispered conversation. During this she asked me where I hoped to work as a staff nurse, and I, of course, said Children's Ward as I loved working there before. She was very interested and started asking if I was there when Prof Calne did the liver transplants. I was proud to say I had nursed the first one, but she was more interested in the second one. In all innocence I explained that sadly that little one had died too, and she burst into uncontrollable tears.

Thinking this was rather an overreaction and worrying we would disturb the patients, I hustled her out to the office and produced a box of tissues. It was a while before she could speak again, and then it all came pouring out that she was the mother of the baby the donor liver was taken from. I felt terrible, almost as if I had killed her baby a second time. How could I possibly have known? She was such a kind lady and said she was glad to know the truth and she was sure it would all help move medical science forward eventually. In contrast I felt totally inadequate as I passed tissue after tissue to her and gave her a hug. Then suddenly we had to go back to the ward as an admission came up and there was work to do.

Now I'm worried about her. Presumably she'll go home to tell her husband and I do hope they can comfort each other. She may not be on our ward tonight, and even if she is she may not speak of it again. At times like this I wonder if we ever get to a stage where we feel confident to cope with all eventualities, probably not.

It seems the whole of our set has an intense attack of the 'fed up' phase and an 'I don't care' attitude. (Oh yes we do!) There have been several arguments as we get on each other's nerves. Heaven help us when October comes. The easiest solution to this is sleeping throughout the day and hardly seeing the others. To be fair, Angie is much happier now she has her car, and it's great to hear her laughing again.

I must try to get some studying done in my nights off.

Letter home:

1st August 1970

The beginning of nights was unbelievably busy with lots of critically ill patients, but they're all sorted out now and it is very quiet. I must say I'm pleased, as if I run on full adrenalin for too long I don't sleep as well. I'm looking forward to coming home to get away from all the talk about work and finals.

I bought Peter a flower power tie to go with his yellow shirt and the new image went down well with his father when his parents visited at the weekend. Peter and I went to see Chekhov's Seagull at the Art's Theatre. The acting was superb, but I was too tired to really understand it.

Paul and Liz are having more wedding discussions. I've offered to make Liz's wedding dress for her as her mother simply does not have the time, but she hasn't taken me up on that yet. I should quite enjoy doing it as I love the pattern she's chosen. I'd like to contribute to making her happier.

1st August 1970

Darling Peter,

The ward has gone eerily quiet now and it makes the weekend seem endless and lonely. Sometimes I wish we were frantically busy and time would pass faster.

I should be more careful what I wish for. The phone rang and we had an admission. It seemed pretty straightforward until the ward orderly whispered, "He's alive, nurse" and it took me a moment to realise he meant fleas! We covered 'checking for infestation' in PTS, but honestly this is the first time I've come across it. The 'gentlemen of the road' that come into Accident Service for a bath in the middle of the night carry a bar of soap in their pockets, but this tramp was more like the meths drinkers we see in the Market Square. Fortunately he was not too ill and we dunked him, clothes and all, into a bath to drown them, peeled the clothes off and left them soaking whilst we moved him to another bath, gave him a good scrub, washed his hair and beard and tackled his finger and toe nails. Not a pretty sight. He was not best pleased, but not too stroppy either, even when I combed the tangles out of his hair and beard. He is all tucked up in hospital pyjamas now looking like a rather sweet old gentleman and snoring gently.

Continued a day later:

I was not amused to find some fleas on me when I started scratching in bed. After a bath, hair wash, clothes wash, uniform change, even a bed change and washing the bed sheets, I succeeded in getting rid of them.

We had fewer staff on tonight and, of course, were busier. Also I seem to have caught a tummy bug or eaten something that has disagreed with me as I've been sick as a dog all night and am feeling somewhat weak and fragile. Hopefully I can sleep it off.

4th August 1970

Last night tonight, thank goodness. Griffith has closed for redecoration and I've moved up to Albert with all the patients. It feels strangely different and the freshly painted smell is not helping my dodgy stomach. I'm feeling much better, but kept going a bit dizzy, so I have restarted solid food. Hopefully I'll be 100 per cent in no time.

I'm going home for nights off, but will come back by train on Friday to be with you. Life at The Nursery is not good. We're all worried about Angie. Her uncle has changed his mind and won't let her keep her car in Cambridge until she is a more experienced driver, which may be sensible, but the car was the one thing keeping her cheerful, and how can she become more experienced with no car? Also ants have invaded the kitchen; fleas by night and ants by day. 'Tis a good job I've got a sense of humour!

Morning is creeping up on us. It is not as misty so the good weather will probably break today, typical.

Written from my parents' house:

5th August 1970

I'm sorry I got het up on the phone tonight. It was so wonderful to hear you and I love you so much. It's mostly because I am worrying about my off duty. I hate having a block of days off in the middle of the week like this because I can't see you and I miss you so much, and then I'll be working when you are on holiday.

Accident Service has a reputation for being really awkward over requests and I don't want to miss my school friend's wedding. I went up to the New Site to try and speak to either of the two sisters, but, of course, neither was on duty. The staff nurses were offhand and no help. All I could do was to leave a pleading letter and pray. It's stressful with all the worrying, the hoping, the pleading and the nauseating buttering up – I hate it. Now I've spoilt our few precious moments on the phone too, sorry. I don't believe anybody could love anyone more than I love you, I just want to be with you.

11th August 1970

Accident Service was frantically busy all my first morning because of the torrential rain and wet roads. One chap had gone through his windscreen and landed on the road in front of his car. He looked like a patient in Emergency Ward 10 on television. I am so glad you always wear your seat belt. He's very lucky as the glass missed his eyes and he'll probably only have minor scars in a few weeks' time, but he looked horrendous when the ambulance men brought him in.

The morning went very fast. I'm starting to understand the routine and think I will enjoy my time here.

Yesterday afternoon was devoted to revision. This morning I went to see our sister tutor, asked lots of questions and gleaned some useful information. I think she really will help all she can and she explained the common reasons for failure, so with a bit of luck I can steer clear of the traps. This afternoon I'm going into the Old Site to get my training record book signed up and see my reports from both Musgrave and Griffith. Funny way to spend time off, but it has to be done.

The next day was 12th August, usually known as the 'Glorious Twelfth', but it was far from that for us. I was on a B shift and looking after a well built middle aged man with burn blisters on his arm and hand. The doctor had asked me to cut the dead skin off and put a clean dressing on the wound. A junior nurse came in and said I had a phone call and to take it quickly. To receive a personal phone call whilst on duty was an unforgivable sin and I couldn't think who would be calling.

It was Peter. He told me his father had committed suicide early that morning. He had hanged himself in the office at the rear of their newsagent's shop. Peter had driven from Sheffield to London and had to identify the body. He sounded traumatised, lost and desperately in need of my help. At the same time the sister was telling me off for taking a private call and all I could do was assure him I would phone him as soon as I was off duty, hang up, apologise to the sister and return to the patient.

As I concentrated on completing the dressing, the patient turned a nasty shade of grey, and despite assuring me he was feeling all right, he passed out and fell from the chair to the floor. Fortunately I half caught him and nothing more was hurt than his pride.

The next day went by in a blur. There were awkward phone calls with me trying to support Peter and him saying virtually nothing as grief seemed to have turned him into a block of ice that no amount of my love could thaw. I went to see the Assistant Matron to request compassionate leave for the funeral on the fourteenth, the next day, which was refused on the grounds we were only engaged and not married and therefore this was not the funeral of a close relative. Oh how I missed the caring, compassionate Miss Puddicombe we had all known and loved and whom I am sure would have been more sympathetic and understanding, but she had retired and already it felt as if attitudes had changed.

I pleaded with the sister on Accident Service to allow me to change my day off and she reluctantly agreed I could, but only if the nurse whose day off it was would swap with me.

Fortunately she was kind and willing. Gill, Angie, Liz and Rita were enormously supportive and Gill lent me a navy dress to wear to the funeral. Luckily it was warm and dry as none of us owned a suitable coat.

The funeral service was in Golders Green and I travelled by train, there and back in the one day as I worked late the night before and had to be back on duty early the next morning. Peter's uncle, his father's brother, was a tower of strength and ushered us all through that dreadful day. Peter's mother appeared oddly unaffected by events, and Peter was still as if untouchable, encased in an invisible shell that I couldn't break through.

I had never been to a Jewish funeral before, but as it was held at the crematorium it was not so different, and the only awkward moment for me was when I noticed the flowers I had sent were on the coffin, which seemed odd. Later it was explained to me that normally there are no floral tributes at Jewish funerals and I concluded that I had done the wrong thing. Even so I was glad that Peter's uncle was kind enough to place them on the coffin. They were dark red roses, simply tied in a bunch, and they softened the sadness, expressing love in that dark hour.

The day seemed to go on forever, and trying to eat dinner in an hotel that evening as if nothing had happened was a nightmare. Despite time stretching out as if every minute was an hour, it was suddenly time for us to part. I remember enveloping Peter in the biggest hug, trying to warm him with my love, but he felt like a solid cold rock and could give nothing back.

I sat on the train and cried for both of us.

The next morning I was summoned to the Assistant Matron's Office and ticked off like a naughty schoolgirl for daring to go to the funeral when my request for compassionate leave had been denied. This was too much. I may have reorganised my day off, but I had done it with Sister's permission and I had then gone to the funeral in my own time. I didn't pause to think, I simply reacted. I felt totally composed and spoke slowly and determinedly.

"And you have the nerve to call this the caring profession?" I asked, turned on my tail, walked out and quietly shut the door behind me. I don't know what I expected to happen next, but nothing did.

I phoned Peter every day, trying my best to support him despite the miles between us, but what with having to use call boxes, working shifts and the inevitable expense, before long I returned to writing.

24th August 1970.

Darling Peter,

You sounded so lost and lonely on the phone last night. I almost wish I could run, run, run away, dragging you with me until we could settle down on our own and I could make you happy again. Sadly running away doesn't solve anything, nor does giving up. Anyway nurses don't run! Somehow we have both got to carry on finding comfort in letters whilst we are apart. Don't be lonely for I am with you. Don't feel lost for I have found you. And don't be miserable or worried because we will solve all the problems and work towards a happily married future together. Believe me, with our love this can happen.

Gill has arrived back in Cambridge with all her twenty-first cards, presents and flowers. She is thrilled to bits with the cameo brooch Henry has given her and it reminded me of how I felt about the cameo ring you gave me. It seems a lifetime ago. Gill's suffering from an acute attack of 'it is ages until we get married'. I know exactly how she feels.

25th August 1970

Liz's twenty-first is next, early September, and fortunately on my nights off. There are plans afoot. Parents will probably take Liz, Paul and us out to dinner near here, maybe that scrumptious place at Eynesbury, on the Friday, and Liz is half planning an impromptu party on the Saturday. Paul suggests we all buy her things from the Denby range of china she

162

wants to collect which seems a sensible idea. I'll go ahead and choose something from the two of us. Paul is teasing her and telling her to get a passport for their honeymoon in case they fly to Paris one weekend.

Gill and I had a big heart to heart last night which helped me a lot. She knows more about our problems than anyone and is a confidential and understanding pair of ears. She really is a good friend to us both and I count myself lucky to have her support. I wish you had a similar friend in Sheffield. At least you can tell me all your troubles, and I hope all my love, hugs, kisses and silent understanding can be of comfort to you. I love you and will always do all I can to help you.

I'm glad to hear you've found a happy photograph of your father to remind you of better times and how he always smiled at you. I was very conscious of your close relationship and saw the knowing looks the two of you exchanged. From the moment I heard of his death I worried about your mother, her paranoia and the difficulties of your relationship with her. I can see the enormity of the situation we have to face. She is a very sick woman who refuses to ask for help and, unless she hurts herself or someone else, she cannot be hospitalised against her will and treated. The situation that developed in her flat last Sunday was bound to happen sooner or later. Thank goodness for my experience at Fulbourn. I still find it hard to believe that my taking a book from the shelf to read provoked such a tirade. I know you said not to touch anything, but I never imagined you meant it that literally. We have to believe that she will improve as her life settles back down. You must let me help as much as I can and together we will take care of her. I think we both need to learn to recognise when trouble is brewing and try to avoid it for her sake, and more importantly for yours.

I guess we can never understand how much the Holocaust affected her, and as she won't talk about it we will never know what she experienced. To have left her mother behind in Vienna and to know subsequently she died in a concentration camp must be a huge burden to carry. Always remember that without her I wouldn't have you. Our love and friendship are the most important things in my life and these troubles can only bring us closer together. I know the loss of your father will always hurt, but I do believe that time will erode the cutting edge of grief eventually.

28th August 1970

I hope you have arrived in London to find things better than you expected and that your mother is coping with the shop.

It would be lovely if you could phone me on nights, and yet this is not without problems. Firstly we must not block the Accident Service line, and secondly Night Sister spends a lot of her time here unless there is a greater need elsewhere. It might be better if I ring you from the call box before I go on. Mostly we will have to rely on letters. I've turned down several invitations so we can stop dashing around and have a quiet time together whilst you are here. A lifetime simply isn't long enough for me to be with you.

30th August 1970

Your fiancée is a very sleepy girl. Nights are going steadily and no major disaster has occurred yet, but I dread that red telephone ringing. The late evenings are usually frantically busy, and then, once we've tidied up and done the necessary cleaning, it goes quiet as the dodo, unless the police are bored too and call in for a chat. I've been doing some studying as it is a good opportunity and I'd be silly to waste the time. Finals are creeping up all too quickly. I can't wait to get them done so that I can move on to all the things I've put on hold until after finals. My life is sleeping, eating, working and studying, all very dull. I'm pleased you and your mother went out with my parents and all was well. I wish I could have been with you.

It has been a strange week on nights. The spasmodic hectic work and contrasting lack of anything to do just does not suit my temperament. Discovering the hospital has done the dirty on me again by sending me to Ward 1 next instead of Children's Ward as I requested puts me in a very unhappy and unsettled frame of mind. Also, of course, all the others have their men here, and it is not much fun going on nights and potentially coping with the victims of road traffic accidents (which, believe me, can be a bit gruesome) when the others are setting off for a party. Then the next morning it is a beautiful sunny day, I have to go to bed, and they are all chatting about the wonderful time they had.

I'm going to the Old Site in the morning to speak to the Nursing Officer in charge of allocation. Then I'll go and see the sister on Children's Ward to try and get her to put in a good word for me. Could she have rejected my request? (Is paranoia catching?) I would hate to feel I wasn't wanted. I am convinced Children's Ward is the right place for me to finish my training. This is very important to me; I have to make it happen.

Please will you wear your new yellow shirt and flower power tie for Liz's twenty-first? Goodness knows what I shall wear as I'm bored with the contents of both my and Gill's wardrobe. Oh dear, I do sound disgruntled. I promise to cheer up before I see you.

7th September 1970

I set out for the hospital to see the Nursing Officer. I failed to track her down so I'll have to try again early tomorrow morning. Ever since Miss Puddicombe left the atmosphere seems to have changed. The new Principal Nursing Officer doesn't start until later this month. Apparently the title Matron is old fashioned and everything is to become more professional. Already there is an overall Chief Nursing Officer for the United Cambridge Hospitals in post. It is all to do with the recommendations of the Salmon Report. Personally I am not convinced this is the right way forward. You can't run a hospital with business managers who don't understand the medical side. The next thing will be nurses wanting to have degrees. That is fine by me, but to move the training into lecture theatres and away from the wards, which has been suggested, is stupid. We'll lose the workforce, and nurses with degrees won't want to get their hands dirty, and that is what nursing is all about. It is a completely different career to being a doctor. It worries me; already the juniors have a different attitude and walk off at the end of a shift whether their share of the work is completed or not, and we seem to use more and more agency nurses who don't know the patients, the wards or the routine. I don't like change when I can't understand the logic. I love this hospital…but I need to staff on Children's Ward!

I arrived on Griffith as the consultant was about to start a nurses' teaching session which I tagged on to as it was an easy form of revision. Sister was busy, but agreed to let Staff Nurse sign my record book, which she did. It has to be completed at the end of my time on each ward recording all the nursing procedures I am now capable of performing proficiently. But Staff Nurse couldn't show me my report so I still haven't seen that. Perhaps our sister tutor can get hold of it for me.

I went up to Musgrave too, and that sister agreed to sign my book if I come back on Thursday afternoon. By then it will be time for me to start pestering Accident Service to sign. What a stupid system. It is things like this that need to be sorted out; there is no need to change the whole management and training structure.

I'm tired, longing for next weekend and cursing my rotten off duty. It makes it hard for you having to wait around for me to come home, and yet it will be truly wonderful to spend those few hours close together in the darkness. Then you will sleep well and I can feel I am helping, even if only by being beside you and surrounding you with love.

A funny thing happened this morning on the way to see the Nursing Officer. I was just about to knock on her door when she came round the corner. I was wondering whether to study the notice board and pretend I hadn't seen her until she was safely inside when she spotted me, recognised me, and said, "Children's on the twentieth."

Well, I nearly fell through the floor in amazement. I could hardly believe it, but pulled myself together and thanked her profusely. Isn't life marvellous? I mean, just think if I'd been five minutes earlier or later I would have looked a right idiot telling my tale of woe when the office had already decided to alter the change list. I am so relieved. It's perfect: Staff Nurse on Children's Ward. I'm positively skipping around.

Angie was delighted for me. Apparently she was sure I would hand in my notice after finals if this didn't work out; she hit the nail on the head there.

Whilst you need to see your mother every other weekend I'll try to arrange my off duty so I work then and have better time off to be with you in between. Not that I get much say in it, but I'll try. I hope this good news heralds a run of better luck for both of us. Fingers crossed your project is going well too and that you get a big salary increase.

Written from my parents' house:

15th September 1970

I've fixed an appointment to see the family doctor as we agreed. I decided to talk to Mother on the way home in the car about going on the Pill and she was very sweet and helpful and assured me most couples don't wait until they are married. Why then are we all taught that you should?

Sis wanted to know why I was going to the doc's. "About my liver," I replied vaguely.

"Oh, going on the pill then? About time too," she quipped, and I had to laugh. She's planning on wearing a black skirt to Liz and Paul's wedding; there's daring.

My little brother, Malcolm, has been in hospital whilst on holiday in France. He says that the nurses there always took his temperature rectally and gave all the drugs by suppositories. Why?

I finally handed in my record book yesterday, all signed and sealed. I've made a long list of every procedure I've ever done so that I can swot up on them because it is rumoured they choose our practical situation from the book.

Gill is installed back in Main Theatres, her favourite place, and she is very cheerful. Rather her than me. Isn't it lucky we all love different aspects of nursing?

Written from my parents' house:

16th September 1970

Well I've seen the doc. He explained my liver will be functioning perfectly normally again now and it is not a contraindication to my going on the Pill. He gave me a fatherly chat: "Are you sure" and "Some men just want their wicked way." Also he emphasised that I will not be safe until after one whole month. How patronising; I am a nurse and not an idiot.

I am pleased the Pill will be possible as I don't fancy any other method of birth control and it is the safest, but (why is my life never easy?) this doc would not prescribe it as he is Roman Catholic! He said to go to Family Planning in Cambridge. I suppose I'll have to try them, but I don't hold out great hopes of success.

The dentist extracted my wisdom tooth, leaving me numb and thirty bob poorer. After that we went round to see Mother's elderly friend for tea. She'd made me another of her delicious fruit cakes, and insists on baking our wedding cakes if we can find someone else to ice them. She is crippled with arthritis, but always so pleased to see me and such a poppet, like an extra granny. I love her.

At bedtime Father came in to see me and said if I've ever got any moral problems I would talk to him, wouldn't I?

168

I replied that of course I would, but I hadn't any problems at the moment as it was all decided. He said yes, he supposed it was, and added, "I'm on your side anyway, you know." Wasn't that sweet of him? I think I'm very lucky to have such understanding parents.

Finals–Staff Nurse

Darling Peter,

Liz has bought a wedding dress and sent off for her passport, hoorah! We all think she'll look lovely. Goodness knows what I'm going to wear.

I'm glad to be leaving Accident Service and heading back to Children's Ward, but I am a bit anxious. Will Sister welcome me back? Will I settle in easily? Will things work out how I hope so that I can see you more?

Today is the beginning of the end of my training and almost the start of a new job. Staffing is very different to being a student: more responsibility, higher expectations and no excuses. These next three weeks until finals are bound to be difficult. I have to warn you I do get very irritable and moody when taking exams, but I promise to try my hardest to do well. I know you are worried about your mother, the shop, the flat, and what with that and your job you have your hands full without having to contend with me and my rubbish off duty as well. I'll miss you quite horribly this weekend, especially as both Paul and Henry will be here highlighting your absence and the weather promises to be glorious too. I do understand your need to go and see your mother.

When people ask the date of the wedding and I say April, they reply, "Oh, quite soon then." I'm trying hard to believe them as I long for that day to come, and I know you do too. I love you, always and forever.

How did I guess that you would be feeling miserable about my off duty? You must understand that it won't miraculously change or improve yet, but at least this sister always does it a whole week in advance. I'm not entitled to staff nurse privileges yet and there are several seniors on the ward at the moment. The senior full time staff nurse is working her notice, so after finals things should definitely look up.

Sister gave me a genuine welcome back and seems pleased to have me. She's briefed me on the staff nurse role on this ward, and I think we shall get on famously. She's very reserved and not an easy person to get to know, but she does run an efficient ward. I think it will be a working relationship rather than a friendship. The staff nurse who is staying on is warmer, but inevitably she and I will always be on different shifts. There is also a lovely state enrolled nurse who has been here ages and is the fount of all knowledge, which she shares helpfully and willingly. She is brilliantly supportive as she quietly handles all the routine jobs quickly and efficiently. I don't know how we'd all cope without her.

Please don't nag me over going on the Pill. I know you must be frustrated and that we agreed it was the right time for us to express our love for each other in greater depth. I don't think you understand how hard it is to get to the Family Planning Clinic when it is only held one evening a week and I can hardly request time off for that reason! I expect they'll quiz me and make me feel embarrassed and might even refuse my request because we are not married yet. I will go. I don't expect you to come with me, but I do need your mental support. With hindsight I should have started all this earlier so that it didn't come on top of finals. I never guessed it would be so complicated and take this long. Sorry.

I'm sorry your mother is being difficult too and not appreciating your efforts to help. You will always know that you have tried your best even if you never get thanked for it. I know it's a cliché, but time will ease things even if that doesn't seem possible at present. I wish I wasn't bogged down with studying at the moment and could help you more. You must feel as if the whole world is against you and that simply isn't true. Try to believe that in a few weeks things will seem a lot less black. I want you and I need you every bit as much as you need me. This is a bad patch, but together we will come through it because our love is definitely strong enough, you'll see.

23rd September 1970

I want to make the most of my time off to be with you this weekend because I know that the following weekend, with finals so close, I shall be horribly touchy. Maybe that would be a good time for you to go and see your mother again.

Yesterday was my day off and I managed to make the nine o'clock revision tutorial which I considered a pretty splendid effort. I studied on my own at the house too, although I have to confess to being caught sound asleep with my head on the textbook.

It's super being back on Children's Ward and I feel much more relaxed and in control of things. On Accident Service I only really enjoyed myself when we had a major trauma come in and the adrenalin was buzzing. Afterwards I found getting my thrills from other people's misfortune somewhat macabre and that didn't feel comfortable.

Sorry I got a bit emotional about the sex thing. It is difficult wanting something so much and having to wait for artificial contraception. I consider that very aptly named, for although recognising the necessity it does rather limit spontaneity and one's natural instincts.

Our exam numbers came yesterday. Do you think 641 sounds lucky?

28th September 1970

Thank you for my box of chocolates and a really lovely weekend. I got the washing done and then settled down to revision until Gill came home. Now I'm having a break to write this letter and go to the nurses' reps meeting with her. This evening I'll do some more studying and save the chocolates for a reward at bedtime. I've a funny feeling this week will fly by, as time has a habit of doing when exams loom.

Exam tension has hit The Nursery. We are all grouchy and you should hear the language! There could be a few rows before the week is out. Thinking optimistically, in two weeks it will be over and the new exciting phase of our lives can start in earnest: planning for our wonderful future together.

30th September 1970

I'm enjoying the delicious chocolates and the others are helping eat them. Fortunately we all have a different favourite one which is probably because we get given so many from grateful patients that we all get a bit choosy. I am trying to work hard, but it is difficult to concentrate. I know I've covered a lot of ground, but I am determined to revise every little thing.

We are busy at work too, but I'm not complaining because I feel I've found my feet on the ward and I love it. I hadn't realised how much I missed the egg sandwiches until they were in front of me again. We make lots for the children's tea, but mostly they fail to appreciate them and they are left for us to devour later in the kitchen, which will be a real bonus when I qualify and have to pay for meals.

As a great favour to the office, and hopefully to my own advantage too, I've agreed to change the dates of my November holiday to two separate weeks, one in January, instead of a straight fortnight. I've requested night duty so that my nights off will come over Liz and Paul's wedding and run up to the first week of holiday. The office did try to persuade me to wait until the New Year for the whole holiday, but I compromised on this solution which should work well for us.

Gill is starting to get really nervous, but is trying hard to hide it. Like me she mostly feels she should pass, and yet has that annoying niggle that keeps saying "You just might fail, it happens". The thought of writing quickly for three hours and then having to do it all again in the afternoon is daunting. A levels seem a long time ago; I'd forgotten how tiring it all is. I shall never take another exam after this one.

Pay day today, but as I have to buy Liz's wedding present, Henry's twenty-first gift and then my new maxi-skirt and boots I shall soon be broke again.

You are right. Our troubles do make our love stronger and bind us closer together. United we can cope with all life throws at us.

5th October 1970

My poor hand is so tired and I'm exhausted as well. At least it is all over. I feel deflated and am experiencing that horrid aura of anticlimax. The tutors thought the medical paper was a gift and the surgical was foul. They both seemed fair enough to me, but, oh dear, how boring. What a waste of time most of our revision was. Anyway if I haven't passed I shall be hopping mad. I feel wrung out, but quietly confident.

I love you.

9th October 1970

My bike conked out. The chain came off and jammed completely and I won't get it back for several days. Meanwhile I am walking and hitching the hospital transport, which is a real drag.

The ward is ultra-quiet. We reached a record low yesterday with only six children and no babies for two hours, but then new admissions rolled in again.

Mother came to visit and I persuaded her to buy something new for Liz and Paul's wedding. I also bought my wedding dress material – well part of it anyway as I need to get the lining later. I know that sounds a bit crazy, but I saw the material and fell in love with it and it helps me to feel less jealous of Liz. It will be a challenge making my own wedding dress and I want plenty of time to ensure perfection; happy thoughts.

I got a message from Henry today to say I should eat more as I'm getting too scraggy, cheeky devil! Following my example of knitting for you, Gill has embarked on a jumper for him. She's using such huge needles her progress is quicker than mine.

Angie, Gill and I answered three adverts for flats in the Cambridge News, but it came to nothing as the landlords wanted tenants immediately. I suppose we shall have to wait until November to look. We are all sad to think we shall be leaving The Nursery because it has been a happy house share.

13th October 1970

The practicals started this morning and everyone is returning with tales of woe, enough to scare anyone, and petrifying me. The examiners seem to be asking all sorts of obscure things not necessarily tailored to our personal experience as we had assumed. I hate having a surname at the end of the alphabet and wish I'd been one of the first instead of last. At least when I marry you that will change. I hate practical exams.

I feel really dopey all the time and keep falling asleep when I get home from work. I suppose it has been ages since I had a holiday and I've had a long run of day duty. I'm longing for a break.

Angie and I, Gill and Henry, went to Harvest Festival. It was a lovely service and reminded me to be jolly thankful for all the happiness I have, especially our love.

I must go and press your jumper and then it is all ready to give to you to help keep you warm in the frozen north until I am married to you, then I can borrow it!

Keep your fingers crossed for me at 11.30am on Thursday.

15th October 1970

My practical went reasonably well and I feel confident I made a good impression even if I did get the left and right sides of the heart confused. I've always had a blind spot about left and right. The situation they gave the two of us was ghastly, but between us we did the right things and certainly got through that part of the questioning credibly. Then I got asked about gastroenteritis in babies – what a gift, I could hardly believe my luck – followed by general chit-chat on geriatrics. If I've failed then I don't deserve to be a nurse.

I came back to the house to find two letters from you and the fantastic news that you can come to Liz and Paul's wedding after all, hoorah. It will be twice as nice with you there.

Now my exams are over, and it hardly seems possible that they really are, it is almost time to see you again. Sister was very sweet about finals, let me off early last night and has been very kind whilst trying to give me confidence. Maybe she really does want me as her staff nurse. I only need one thing to complete my happiness: you by my side.

20th October 1970

It is freezing cold and I've got a runny nose and sore throat and feel like hibernating and never leaving my warm bed ever again.

I filled in my General Nursing Council questionnaire this morning which was a huge effort and took forever, and when I've finished this letter I'll have to brave the wind and rain to the post box and get some shopping as the cupboard is bare. Only seven nights to get through and I'll be on holiday. It will be good to get right away and relax.

It's very quiet with only three of us at the house, shades of things to come, but I get more done; less chatting and drinking coffee. My Godmother has sent a guide book of Cyprus for me to give to Paul secretly. So now we know their honeymoon destination. I am delighted Paul has booked something special and I'm sure Liz will be thrilled. I must cut out my new skirt and waistcoat this afternoon or it will never be finished in time. Meanwhile I must eat something or there is a risk I shall fade away completely on night duty and there'll be nothing left for you to cuddle.

23rd October 1970

My first two nights whizzed by in a whirl of activity. Then we were quieter, which gave me a chance to get more organised, feel more in control and happier. We've got lots of wonderful children in and some lovely, cuddly babies. I feel at home and glad to be back in the old routine. It's great to know I won't get moved about any more and Sister treats me very well.

The sad saga of the Pill continues. Despite my friend's experiences earlier in the year I tried Family Planning, as the GP suggested, reasoning we are engaged and the wedding is quite soon. Sadly not soon enough because they promptly said, "Come back in March" and showed me the door. I should have fibbed. Why am I so honest? In desperation I found a call box and telephoned the Youth Advisory Centre and now I wish I'd thought of that in the first place. They have a Birth Control Clinic in Clarendon Street and I fixed an appointment. I duly turned up at 11.10am yesterday, missing precious sleeping time to be there, only to be told the receptionist had booked me on the wrong day and could I come again next week! Fortunately it seems a pleasant 'strictly confidential' sort of place with helpful staff. It is a private clinic and the consultation costs £4 plus a further 8s a month for the pills. It seemed ridiculously expensive until I overheard that an abortion is at least £150! Anyway you'll be pleased to know I haven't given up and have booked in again for next week.

I've made a good start on my sewing and I'll search for a cheap trendy hat on my nights off. Angie and Rita are sunning themselves in Spain, lucky them.

My outfit consisted of a short straight skirt and a long line waistcoat made from patterned needlecord in autumnal colours: greens, reds and browns. I wore it with a long sleeved white shirt and a sludge green hat with a floppy brim, all very fashionable. The big day, 30th October, dawned fair and there was chaos at my parents' house as too many people tried to get ready at the same moment in too few bathrooms. Mother's new dog, a rough collie, raced around barking excitedly and getting underfoot whilst we tried to decide who was travelling in which car. Paul had a reputation for missing wedding services and only turning up in time for the reception, but today was going to be different and I was determined he would be at Epping Registry Office in good time to await his bride.

At 2.30pm Liz arrived with her family, looking nervous but happy. She was wearing a simple short sleeved white mini-dress and a navy hat which was understated and perfect for the occasion. Beside her Paul looked unusually smart in his only suit. The ceremony was short and sweet as they exchanged their vows and were duly pronounced man and wife. It was a special moment to watch my much loved brother marry one of my dear friends and soon we were all clattering down the stairs and outside onto the grass where we threw huge handfuls of confetti over them with joyous abandon. The reception was held at the Stilton Room in Chingford where we tucked into tea, sandwiches and cake. In no time champagne was passed round ready for the speeches, which I missed as Liz had given me her handbag to hold and I was busy stuffing it secretly with spare confetti. Whilst Paul and Liz said their goodbyes to family and friends, Peter and I were outside persuading the chauffeur Paul had hired to take them into central London to let us decorate the 'going away' car with balloons and streamers. We had to work quickly, but by the time they emerged from the building the car was suitably and colourfully adorned. We waved and waved until they were out of sight, accompanied by toots from the cars of total strangers delighted to join in the festivities.

Peter and I drove back to spend the night at my parents' house. Usually after the excitement of a wedding I feel a sense of anticlimax, but not this time. Oh no, love was in the air and we were happily discussing plans for our own wedding.

Written from my parents' house:

2nd November 1970

Darling Peter,

Thank you for driving all the way from Wales to be at the wedding with me. Liz and Paul looked fabulously happy and I bet they have a super time in Cyprus. It was very emotional watching them get married, but it makes April seem very near knowing that we are next in the queue hammering on the door of married life. This weekend I've felt closer to you than ever before and more in love than I ever knew it was possible to be.

I've fixed an appointment to see the new rector this evening, as you know the retired one replied that he can't come back to marry us as it would not be fair to this chap. Mother's done nothing but talk about April ever since we waved Paul and Liz off. I think we made a brilliant job of decorating the car and the chauffeur was a good sport to let us; it looked perfect as it pulled away into the traffic. I wonder how long it was before Liz found all that confetti I had stuffed in her handbag.

Now I'm determined to get our wedding date, and the church, fixed.

3rd November 1970

Nothing is ever simple! Fortunately Father decided to come with me to see the rector. The conversation went smoothly until I mentioned your family are Jewish and asked if it was possible to keep the wording of the service to God and omit Christ and the Holy Spirit. He got quite stroppy and told me to go and get married in a synagogue! I was upset and tearful because I couldn't believe he was overlooking how kind and considerate it was of you to agree that the ceremony could be in our church. I couldn't understand why he couldn't see what a big concession that was.

Father was his usual calm self and quietly waited until it was obvious the conversation was going round in circles and

179

the rector was not going to budge. Then Father, in his best barrister's voice, pointed out that my name is on the electoral roll of the church and I have a legal right to get married there and if he wasn't prepared to take the service then perhaps your College Chaplain could come and marry us. It turned out the rector knows Canon Duckworth from his own Cambridge days and he reluctantly agreed he will write to him, pointing out that we can use the church, but he will not be present himself as he disapproves. I think we should speak to the Canon first, and if he agrees then hopefully we can settle on a form of service that suits him and us and is legal. I'm a bit worried about it all and shall be relieved when it is sorted out. At the same time I'm glad because I would like to be married in our church and have the reception at my childhood home, but I'd much rather be married by the Canon, whom I adore and respect, than by a stranger who condemns our relationship. Fingers crossed. I shall still love you for ever and ever wherever, however and whenever we do get married.

4th November 1970

So, I waited three long days to phone you at the time we agreed and even cut short a phone call with my school friend, and where were you? Was it a good rugby match? Did you have a few pints as well? I hope you felt horribly guilty when you realised you had forgotten me. I can't find it in my heart to be cross because you have been working so hard and I had a lovely chat with your Welsh landlady. She has a lilting musical accent that I could have listened to for hours. I love the thought of your guilty face when she tells you I rang: you owe me lots of apologetic kisses.

9th November 1970

I spoke to Welfare at the hospital today and they've no suitable accommodation on their books for the three of us, but I ascertained a Syrian doctor and his family are taking over this house on 1st December so we'll have to go somewhere else.

I was welcomed back from holiday yesterday to discover I was fifteen minutes late on duty. No one told me we've started working new hours. Sister said it has been chaos and she is relying on me to get things more organised. I suppose that is a compliment. I've got to go back on nights towards the end of the month, which is fair enough but means I'll be on nights when finals' results come out. Also it looks as if Angie, Gill and I will all be on nights when we move house.

I'm the only one here at the moment and this morning I slept through the alarm and was nearly an hour late to work. As it is at least three years since I last overslept no one was cross, except me with myself. I've set all five alarm clocks to ensure I wake up tomorrow!

11th November 1970

I decided to stick all the Green Shield Stamps in the books and my mouth tastes foul from all the licking, but we have got nearly eight books full already.

Even better, I've found a house for 1st December: a huge achievement. Guess who the neighbours are – we shall be living bang smack next door to the Eightsome, imagine that! Yes, our new address will be 15, Caius Terrace, Glisson Road. It's like a dolls' house compared to The Nursery, but is a lovely mid-terrace cottage where you enter through the front door straight into the living room, which is small and easy to heat. The kitchen has a little table with four chairs and essentials like the cooker and fridge. The bathroom and loo are by the back door, as in most of these old terraced houses, and inevitably it will prove to be damp too; the fresh coat of whitewash looks suspicious to me. Hidden behind a door in the kitchen is a steep, narrow staircase mounting to one single room and one double with two single beds. Gill and I will continue sharing. Rent will still be 13gns each a month and it looks as if running expenses will be similar too. The lease is for six months, which is perfect, but sadly there is no telephone. Probably just as well as we couldn't really afford it. Suddenly the whole business of having to sort out, pack and move becomes a reality and a bit of a nightmare really as we must leave this place spick and span to get our deposit back. At least with the Eightsome next door we shall never be lonely.

New working hours mean a B shift is now one o'clock to nine o'clock, which is an improvement. Half days are the same as before and split shifts are longer, which will be horrible.

Written from my parents' house:

17th November 1970

Darling Peter,

I arrived here on Sunday to find Paul and Liz gloriously tanned and full of stories reliving their wedding and honeymoon. It must be a huge anticlimax having to return to work. I notice Mother has stopped calling me 'Lizzy' like she always did before and now I am 'Eileen' to save confusion. It sounds to me as if I've been naughty and I'm not sure I like it, but I suppose I'll have to get used to it.

Apparently the chauffeur, in the spirit of the occasion, did not stop for them to remove the streamers, balloons and 'just married' sign and took them like that all the way to the hotel in central London. Full marks to him! Liz never opened her handbag until she needed a hanky half way through their meal in the revolving restaurant of the Post Office Tower and the confetti spilt out all over the place. Fortunately she saw the funny side and they were given complimentary after dinner drinks as a wedding present. I was impressed Paul had arranged to take her there as it will have cost him a small fortune; the views must be spectacular. It is lovely to know my brother does have a romantic side, though he's kept it well hidden until now.

Mother and I are going shopping tomorrow so I can look at china and glass and decide what we should add to our wedding list. Mother's bought some of the new polyester and cotton sheets and I wonder if they wash and wear as well as they claim to. I do hope so because nylon sheets feel horrible and I hate them.

24th November 1970

Darling Peter,

We are all quite enjoying this moving lark, thank goodness for Angie's car. We collected a pile of empty boxes from the hospital and are rapidly filling them. The pile for the dustbin men looks like Mount Everest and we fully expect one of them to have a coronary and need resuscitation. I've bought a padlock for my staff nurse's locker on Children's Ward so I can keep more spare uniforms there. It feels a great privilege to have my very own locker after all this time, and working with children means frequent changes of apron as they are delightfully messy darlings and we need to look clean, hygienic and efficient at all times. Parents are surprisingly impressed by a clean pinny; it boosts their confidence in us. Sounds silly, but it is true.

I did some tidying in the garden this morning and am about to experiment with one of those new spray oven cleaners to tackle the months of grease. Next time I see you we will be in the new house. It feels like the end of an era here and I know we shall all be a bit sad to close the door the last time.

Looking forward I've bought a 1971 diary and written the date of the wedding in!

26th November 1970

As I grow more and more nervous about the results I wish that you were here to hold my hand. It's the candlelit service at Great St Mary's Church this Sunday and I'm sad we shall not be there together for the last time. In many ways it is miserable to think we are nearly at the end of our Cambridge days, but then a great feeling of joy comes over me to think that also means our wedding day draws ever nearer.

All these lightning postal strikes are worrying – suppose our results get held up. There will be lots of us on nights all getting wound up together. At the moment work is going well and we've got some super children in. The ward is quiet and there is lots of time to play with them, which is fun. My maternal instincts are being well and truly stimulated. Lucky I'm on the Pill now!

Do you remember the little boy who was run over by a lorry whom I nursed when I was on Children's Ward before? He is making marvellous progress and has started trying to walk again. The healing capacity of children is amazing. He can manage his own colostomy, and otherwise everything is pieced back together and working, and even the skin grafts look good now. He comes with me every morning when I take the ward report to Night Sister's office. I push the wheelchair and he 'drives' his remote controlled car along the empty corridor in front of us, executing an impressive three point turn when we get there and then we return to the ward at top speed.

We continue to turn The Nursery back into number 33. It is beginning to look very bare and nondescript and not like our home at all. I'm looking forward to our cosy new abode, making it ours and settling into a nice little rut there for a few months. I love cottages, they suit me.

29th November 1970

What a night we've had! I never realised so many people throughout the hospital knew me and cared about my passing finals: registrars, doctors, sisters, nurses, orderlies, porters, maids and even a couple of consultants. I never before appreciated how much part of a team we all are. We were conspicuous in our new tall hats, and the congratulations poured over us from all sides. If only the whole set had passed it would have been fantastic fun. It has taken a lot of hard work to keep Angie and Dawn cheerful, and at one point it looked as if the difference between passing and failing could put a terrible strain on friendships.

I devoted the night to 'public relations' and by morning all of us were joking away at breakfast like the loyal friends that we still are. I think everyone realises that hats and belts and little bits of paper are really insignificant beside the mutual respect, admiration and comradeship between those of us who were lucky and those who weren't. In no time at all February will be here, Dawn, Angie and Rita will have passed resits and we'll all be staff nurses together.

Dawn was on nights on Private Ward (immediately above Children's Ward) and we knew she would get her result first as she had it posted home where the post arrives very early, and her mother was to open it and phone instantly. One of her nurses rushed down to warn me she had failed and I felt paralysed with shock. It is well recognised that Dawn is the most dedicated nurse in the set and my mind was grappling with the implications that surely then we had all failed. Two minutes later I was legging it upstairs to give her a hug. A miscarriage of justice if ever there was one. And why did Angie fail? She shouldn't have as she is a wonderfully caring and gentle nurse. Why Rita too? I guess nerves must have got the better of them.

Strangely the hospital grapevine went into overdrive and the word got round that I had failed. The poor juniors were anxiously waiting for me, wondering what to say, and then I bounced in with my new hat precariously balanced and secured with a lot of white grips and they cheered. I may be bouncy, but Liz is like a kangaroo. There's no keeping her feet on the ground and it is very infectious.

Tomorrow I'll draw out six guineas and send off for my registration. The ladies on Angie's ward are clubbing together to pay her re-entry fee; a spontaneous vote of confidence that should help to boost her morale.

The best bit about passing was to hear you happy on the other end of the phone line. I wish you could have been here, I felt horribly jealous of Liz and Paul, Gill and Henry, celebrating together. Liz is sitting on cloud nine being state registered and married too. I'm close behind so she'll have to move over and make room for me too. The patients will tell you that we are angels!

Mother came to visit yesterday and brought me a parcel labelled 'To Eileen, for being a clever girl'. Inside was a fish slice, a spoon, a soup ladle and a spud masher, all with matching wooden handles. They are to start life in the house here and then for us in our future home. Wasn't that a kind thought?

When Mother drove off taking Liz to start her journey into married life waves of tiredness and sadness crashed over me. I missed you desperately and April seemed too far away. I went to bed and cried myself to sleep.

Today I feel cheerful and positive again. The cottage is looking very homely, and despite the creeping mildew in the bathroom (I was right) it will be very cosy living here. The hot water works well and the paraffin heater is doing a grand job heating the lounge. We left 33 the cleanest it has ever been. The landlady gave us £19 of the deposit back which should cover the electricity bill, Angie's petrol expenses as removal man and leave us with a little pocket money each.

Life as a staff nurse has been great so far, and I am developing a taste for Ovaltine Rusks dipped in tomato soup for supper, but I wonder if it will be as good on day duty. I shall be the only one of our household at the Post Registration Course, which is sad, but Gill is coming to Prize Giving so at least we can get our hospital badges together.

It does alter the attitude of doctors when we wear a high hat. Our handsome houseman asked my Christian name and calls me Staff Nurse Eileen, which seems to be catching on and I rather like it. We'd never get away with such informality on the other wards, but somehow working with children makes it acceptable, though I'm not sure Sister approves.

I was going to write earlier and catch the last post. I was going to do my ironing, washing, write home and sign all my Christmas cards, but the lights went out for two and a half hours. Fortunately Rita arrived to visit and brought her bicycle lamp in, and then Henry turned up with a candle. Apparently there was a big fire in a shoe shop in town, but I'm not sure the two incidents are connected.

The course went well today; nothing new, but the tutors made it interesting and the time flew by. There were only fifteen of our original set taking part, incredible when you think fifty of us started three years and three months ago.

9th December 1970

The lack of electricity is becoming a bore; it keeps going off for hours at a time. Getting up and trying to get dressed in the pitch black is not funny, especially when it is freezing cold; at least we can't see the ice patterns all over the inside of the window panes! Fortunately the hospital has not been affected so far.

When both Gill and I were getting ready for bed last night we realised that it was the first time that had happened in ages. Of course we got chatting; there was a lot to catch up on, and we didn't get to sleep until the early hours.

The course is proving interesting, and today three of us solved a logistics problem so that it was simpler, with less time taken and less movement, than the result the 'expert' work study team had arrived at. Perhaps they should ask us in future. We gave the superannuation man a run for his money too. He graciously agreed that I will be out of pocket because the scheme is compulsory and I shall not get back all the money I have paid in, but he would not admit it is unfair!

14th December 1970

I seem to write less and less often now that I can afford to phone, but I wanted to say thank you for a delicious dinner and you made me feel gorgeous and very attractive. I love you and enjoy being spoilt. My twenty-second birthday has been a special time and I don't feel any older at all. Parents are buying me an Edwardian silver belt buckle, part of my staff nurse status which they know I want and can't afford. I shall wear it proudly.

The power cuts hit the hospital in the form of reduced voltage. The machines didn't cut out, they just went haywire, which is even more annoying as we had to keep readjusting the controls and keep a close eye on them. Now I must sew nametapes into my new high hats so that I can send them to the hospital laundry to be starched. I love wearing them as they are such a symbol of achievement, but to be honest they are a bit of a hazard on Children's Ward. If the houseman and I lean over a baby's crib at the same moment his head knocks my hat sideways, toddlers take delight in grabbing it, and the ultimate was the other day when I climbed inside an oxygen tent to calm a distressed youngster and the humidity caused the starch to collapse. I emerged half an hour later when the child was asleep looking decidedly like a drunk nurse in some Dickensian novel! I envy the sisters their little lace caps and white cuffs that cover where they have literally rolled their long sleeves up to help. I wonder if rolling her sleeves up feels as symbolic to Sister as I feel about letting my hair down when I come off duty.

16th December 1970

It was a tough day at work today with two little lads who were admitted from the Ida Darwin Hospital recently. One of them I have met before; he has hydrocephalus, but never had a shunt put in to drain the fluid and his head is unbelievably enormous. As he cannot lift it he lies in one of the big cots all the time and it takes two nurses to turn it for him at regular intervals so that he gets a change of view and no pressure sores. Despite this he is a cheerful chap and loves to sing 'Yellow Submarine'. For the rest of my life I shall think of him whenever I hear that tune. He is responding well to yet another course of antibiotics and should be going back to his other home soon. The other children don't seem to notice how strange he looks and chatter with him, which is heart-warming to watch.

The other little boy was dying. His parents had said he was not to be treated and he has a severe chest infection. I phoned his father to warn him that death was near and he came in to visit. It turned out he is a vet and we had a very interesting chat. His wife cannot cope with the heartbreak and she hasn't seen the lad since he was a baby. He was severely brain damaged at birth, can't even recognise his parents, is spastic and is five years old now. The father left and said he wouldn't visit again, but please would I phone him when it was all over. The child died this afternoon and I looked after him myself and carried him round to the mortuary, feeling it was important that someone showed him love even if he couldn't respond. I kept thinking about what his father said about how animals are treated compared to the way we treat humans. Maybe years ago he should have been lovingly put down like a family pet.. Would that have been better? How do you choose who should die and who shouldn't? I don't know.

Sorry, I guess all that sounds a bit morbid. Let's think about Christmas instead. I'm pleased your mother has agreed to go to my parents' house with you and I can't wait to see you on Boxing Day and be in your arms again.

Christmas came and I was once again on night duty. It was preferable to have a trained nurse in charge at night as children can become seriously ill very quickly, and it suited me because it gave me blocks of nights off to be with Peter and I have always loved being up at night when most people are asleep. The dark creates a special feeling of calm and comradeship that I enjoy.

Whenever possible children are sent home for Christmas, and I remember that we had only four boys, two of whom were babies, in the ward on Christmas Eve. We had been inundated with gifts, mostly cuddly toys, for the poor children in hospital, but these children all came from good homes and had plenty of their own presents. Even so they each received a pillowcase full from the mountain of donations. Some were kept to replace ward toys and the remainder passed on to local charities. A consultant, dressed as Father Christmas, travelled the corridors, visiting the wards on a trolley transformed into a sleigh, with an elf and a fairy sportingly played by two press-ganged housemen. There was much ringing of a hand bell, tinsel and a choir of nurses (wearing capes with the red lining side out) singing carols. There was also a fair bit of alcohol consumed, and this year a slightly concussed fairy, whose head had got in the way of the bell, was put to bed in a side ward and quietly monitored with no ill effect.

I stayed up to join in the frivolity and then cycled home to an empty house to get some sleep. A wave of emotion crashed over me as I walked into the cottage leaving me homesick and a little sorry for myself. Gill and Angie had left a bunch of anemones in a vase by my bed, a touching gesture that reduced me to sobs of self-pity! Doubtless I was overtired and I slept soundly.

I returned to work early, feeling fine again and looking very jaunty with silver tinsel around the brim of my high hat and three of the anemones pinned like the Prince of Wales Feathers adorning the front. By Boxing Day morning they were wilting and so was I, but I came off duty feeling fantastic as Peter was there to meet me and whisk me away to my parents' house. Peter's mother was with my family, looking slightly bewildered by a very Christian celebration of Christmas, but not unhappy and she was glad to be included.

Christmas 1970 was the first time all mail was stamped with 'Please use the post code', and for the first time post codes appear on the envelopes of our correspondence, despite the fact that few sorting offices had automated systems, even though my brother Paul was working hard installing them.

Darling Peter,

It seems ages since I put pen to paper to tell you how much I love you. The ward has been ridiculously busy with one of the babies critically ill and doing frightening things to keep us on our toes.

Mother came yesterday for my day off and we had a long chat, mostly about the wedding, of course. My sister has chosen the colour she'd like as bridesmaid, which is fine by me, but we'll need to choose the material together as I'm making the dress. She doesn't want it to look too bridesmaidy. The invitations are on order, lots of them because Father will only send joint invitations to married couples so all our engaged friends will get separate ones. It seems a bit old fashioned to me, but I suppose it is up to him. The photographer is booked and we are chatting up the organist and the verger to get them on side as they are both a bit unsettled by the rector's attitude. The organist looked down his nose at the wedding march from the Sound of Music, but he will play it and it sounds magnificent. The verger has reluctantly agreed we can sign the register in the chancel instead of in the vestry at the rear of the church, which will be so much quicker and better and give us the opportunity to leave church to the traditional Mendelssohn by the main aisle between all our family and friends. It will be perfect.

Mother and I decided assorted spring flowers would look prettiest. The greengrocer is going to buy them at Covent Garden when he goes for his vegetables, and Mother's friends will arrange them. The local florist will arrange my bouquet, the bridesmaid's basket of flowers, corsages for our mothers and the buttonholes. Mother's found someone to ice the cake and I've chosen to have a round one with three tiers. Mother is hiring the china and glass so it all matches and intends to do the catering herself to keep costs down. There seem to be plans for every eventuality; you just have to turn up on the day!

I've nearly finished my evening dress for the company do and I plan to buy you a matching red dicky bow and cummerbund because they look so smart. I'm longing to be with you and to be dancing in your arms.

The early days of January flew by with night duty and then a trip to Sheffield to attend the International Computers' Annual Dinner Dance. It was held at the Grosvenor Hotel on Friday 15th January and I was pleased to meet some of Peter's colleagues and their wives (who were to become our friends when we were married). We dined on asparagus soup, rainbow trout *meunière*, sirloin steak in red wine sauce, Charlotte Royale, cheese and coffee. The drinks were included and I recall there were plenty of them – even whole bottles of brandy, whisky and port left on the tables!

The next day we visited Peter's uncle and aunt in Leeds. They welcomed me as part of the family and I grew very fond of them both.

20th January 1971

What gossip? Angie has given up men and taken up smoking. Gill sends her love. Your beloved fiancée has never worked so hard in all her life.

I didn't stop all morning; no hope of a coffee break. Nine children were admitted overnight and three of them are seriously ill. The consultant turned up to do his round at a ridiculously early hour, at which point I discovered that no one had put the children's names on the end of the cots and I had to check the wrist bands to identify them, which looked as if I didn't know what I was doing. The phone rang all morning at two minute intervals and I swear I spoke to each of the parents at least three times. I managed to keep cool under pressure and I suppose it is all good experience.

I'm starting to realise I shall be very sad to leave this ward and shall miss the regulars that I've got to know, like the children with haemophilia or leukaemia who come in frequently for treatments and the girl who has been enormously courageous when all her skin peeled off after an allergic reaction to chickenpox. Some children suffer so much, but seem to take it in their stride and put up with all sorts of painful procedures very bravely. I've discovered that as long as I am perfectly honest with them I can get their trust. It's no good saying, "Just a little prick" for an injection as they know that is a lie. I've found it is better to say, "Can you be brave? This will hurt for a minute, but will help to make you better", and then promptly ask them a more cheerful question whilst I get on with it and give them lots of praise afterwards.

Did you realise it is two years since I became convinced I could never be really happy without you beside me, and every single day since then I've become more and more certain of that fact? There is nothing now I want more than for 17th April to come quickly so I can be your wife.

We bought our wedding rings in Cambridge on 27th February. Peter's was the more expensive! Then we walked from Midsummer Common along the tow path to watch the Lent Bumps, where we were nearly mowed down by the Canon on his ancient bicycle, peddling furiously and shouting through a megaphone at his crew. In March I commenced a flurry of dressmaking as I stitched my sister's bridesmaid's dress and then my bridal gown, a new dress for my mother, a going-away dress (I bought the coat) and six other new dresses, one for each evening of the honeymoon. This ensured I had enough clothes for married life when I could no longer borrow from Gill's wardrobe.

Peter, not wishing to be described as 'a bachelor of a parish' because he didn't belong to any church, did not want to have our banns called. This meant we had to apply for a special licence, which proved easier than we had feared because it turned out Gill's father was the church official I had to go and see and he was very helpful. Then there was lots more night duty, an arrangement that suited both me and the ward sister.

I have met such a special girl. When I first saw her I wondered why we had admitted a very pregnant teenager. During hand-over I learnt she is twelve and took herself to the GP as she was tired of being teased by her schoolmates and she knew she couldn't possibly be pregnant.

She has a huge ovarian tumour. Surgeons operated and removed as much as they could. Last night I was keeping an eye on her as she was post-op and had been a bit sick after the anaesthetic. When I realised she was awake I went over to see if she wanted a drink or anything. She said she wanted me to answer a question, and then out it came.

"Have I got cancer?"

I wasn't sure what to say and so asked her why she thought that. Unsurprisingly she had overheard the doctors talking at the end of her bed and was clever enough to work out that CA meant cancer.

"Tell me," she demanded. I wasn't sure what the party line was in these cases as I had never come across this situation with a child before, but something in her face told me that only the truth would do. I confirmed she was correct and CA was shorthand for cancer.

"Am I going to die?" she asked in a very mature way, sounding more curious than frightened.

I told her the same as I always say to adults: "We are all going to die one day and none of us can know exactly when. The doctors are doing everything they can to help you", but this time I added, smiling, "But it definitely won't be tonight and it is safe for you to go back to sleep so you can enjoy tomorrow." Then I sat with her, held her hand and stroked her hair. She snuggled down looking reassured and drifted off quite quickly.

In the morning she was perky and asking for breakfast. I told Sister of our conversation and she confirmed my approach was right. I had felt comfortable handling the situation and realised that 'never give false hope, but always

194

be honest and as reassuring as is possible' was a guideline I had followed instinctively, spontaneously and naturally. The incident made me aware of how much I have learnt over the years and that I feel at home and confident as Staff Nurse Eileen. I wish I could stop thinking about her and that I didn't feel so angry that her parents and teachers had turned a blind eye when anyone could see she needed help, whether she had been pregnant or not. She's only a little girl. I hope they will all look after her now; she can't possibly live much longer. She is a beautiful child and it seems desperately unfair. I shall never forget her.

There was a substantial increase in my pay packet now I was a staff nurse, and although I could no longer have free meals at the hospital there were plenty of tins of soup, sliced bread and eggs on Children's Ward for illicit middle-of-the-night snacks. More significantly, I could afford to phone home and phone Peter, so the letters become few and far between.

On Thursday 18th March the Annual Presentation of Certificates took place at the Education Centre at the New Site. Sherry was served and we duly received our certificates and hospital badges. Our hospital badges were bronze, only the older sisters had silver ones, but more importantly our badges were hugely valued as symbols of what we had achieved and a representation of our loyalty to our hospital.

18th March 1971

Darling Peter,

I adore being Staff Nurse Eileen. I feel the part with my high hat, silver belt buckle and hospital badge. Every day is different here: often exciting, but always deeply satisfying. I shall miss Children's Ward when I leave and it will always occupy a place in my heart. I hope I can find an equally special ward to work on in Sheffield.

Thank goodness the postal strike has finished. I know we don't write as often, but it is still wonderful to find a letter waiting when I open the front door. Thank you. Needless to say most of my post is about the wedding and I have bought lots of pretty notelets to make a start on all the thank you letters.

We have a nine-year-old boy in at the moment with school phobia. Sadly the social worker discovered the root of the problem is the father abusing the mother and the boy thinks he can stop this happening if he stays at home with her. We hope to provide a safe haven for him whilst social services sort out the home environment, and he is having lessons on the ward with some of the other children to improve his reading and sums. The plan is to start him back to school from here and then eventually to return him home if the situation there can be sufficiently improved. I do hope so because he is such a lovely, kind child and he doesn't deserve to have such overwhelming worries at his age. He was very withdrawn on admission, but is calm and happy again most of the time. Sadly, but understandably, he gets very distressed when his mother leaves after visiting.

I've been to the finance office and hope that my notice and pay are all finally settled. I've made my last rent payment on this house and have only my share of the gas and electricity bills left to square up.

1st April 1971

I can hardly believe this is my last stint of night duty here on Children's Ward. Maybe my last night ever now we have decided I will work part-time, Monday to Friday, after we are married. I'm sure my new life with you in Sheffield will be full of new experiences to compensate for all I must leave behind me here, but I can't imagine a life without nursing. It is so much a part of who I am and my time in Cambridge has moulded the person I shall always be. I have to admit I shall miss Children's Ward: the cuddles with the babies, that clean smell of Milton in the steriliser, the warm mixture of milky burps and talcum powder – and yes, I'll even miss the dirty nappies! I love the toddlers: carrying an unsettled one on my hip whilst

I take the doctor round and feeling his chubby hands touch my face; wiping their snotty noses and hearing them chuckle when I tickle them and blow raspberries on their tummies. The older children are so brave, spending hours without their parents and accepting medicines and treatment with stoicism. It is fun to read them bedtime stories before I tuck them up at night and see their faces light up when their mothers appear in the morning. I wish there were better facilities so that more parents of very sick children could stay at the hospital. I hope that will happen with the move to the New Site. It's strange to think that soon Children's Ward, as I have known and loved it, will not exist. I hope the New Site manages to recreate the same warm, caring atmosphere that seems to surround the cots and beds here. The ward always feels full of hope, despite the fears and tragedies that are inevitable. Gosh, but I'm sounding very philosophical!

Mother is coming to get me, and nights off at home will disappear fast in a whirl of finalising wedding plans, then rushing back to spend the weekend with you before my last few days of work. I shall leave Cambridge a week before the wedding to help Mother with preparations at home; she has so much to do and I don't want her to be too overtired and not enjoy the big day. I'll phone you as often as I can and count the days down until I will be beside you, always and forever. Not long now!

I spent my last few days on Children's Ward on day duty in a chaotic and hectic rush of admissions and discharges. At one time the ward was so full of cots and beds that we could hardly move between them. The new houseman relied heavily on my knowledge and experience and between us we coped. He had a great sense of humour and took the frenetic pace in his stride. On the round one morning we stopped at the cot of a little girl we had admitted the evening before with Pyrexia of Unknown Origin: a dangerously high temperature that needed investigation. Her temperature had come down overnight, and as I pulled her

197

nightgown up for the doctor to listen to her chest and heart we both realised she was covered in unmistakeable chickenpox spots. His horrified face was so comical I burst out laughing.

"What do we do now?" he asked.

"Discharge her as soon as possible before she infects the whole ward," I said, scooping her up and carrying her away from the other children and into Sister's office. "Bring the cot!"

My last morning was ridiculously busy, and I left the ward eventually about an hour later than I should have. I walked into Sister's office to leave her a note I'd written saying 'goodbye and thank you', only to discover there were coffee cups laid out with a plate of cakes from Fitzbillies, the students' favourite sticky bun shop. The rest of the staff must have planned for a civilised coffee break and a small surprise goodbye party, but we had never even had time to think about stopping. There was a gift wrapped present for me, which I took, and I expect the afternoon staff devoured the cakes later. No one said goodbye. I didn't cry. I cleared my locker for the last time, walked out to collect my bike and cycled away from a very special ward in a wonderful hospital. I had arrived in Cambridge over three years ago as a young, nervous, inexperienced student, and now I was leaving as a confident, mature, trained nurse. It was as simple as that. Addenbrooke's Hospital had become a place I considered home, where I belonged and felt happy working with so many dear friends, and I would miss all of it. I felt as if I had been deeply engrossed in a good book, but had reached the end of the chapter and needed to tear myself away, reluctantly, to attend to mundane everyday matters. I had peeked ahead and knew the next chapter started with a description of the wedding, but I didn't know the detail. I was eager, with the impatience of youth, to reopen the book and become reabsorbed so that I could live every moment and discover how the story developed in future chapters. Meanwhile I had lots to think back on, memories that would live within me forever, together with the patients that entered my heart, never to leave.

What Happened Next

Peter and I were married by his College Chaplain, Canon Noel Duckworth, in a beautifully and especially written service in the church of my childhood on 17th April 1971. After an almighty thunderstorm the night before, the day dawned calm and sunny, as perfect as any bride could wish for, and we were able to have the reception on the lawns at my parents' house exactly as I had hoped. Later the middle tier of the wedding cake was sent to the Children's Ward for my colleagues to enjoy, sharing in a small part of our happiness.

We started married life in Sheffield and I worked part-time on the Special Care Baby Unit in the Maternity Department at Nether Edge Hospital, where both Katherine and Timothy, our first two children, were born. In 1977 we moved to the Chilterns and I trained as an antenatal teacher for the National Childbirth Trust and taught nearly 600 couples over a ten year period. Our third child, Jennifer, was born at home. Peter advanced rapidly up the career ladder and this enabled me to be a fulltime wife, mother, and now grandmother to our five gorgeous grandchildren who are a source of great joy. My spare time was, and still is, spent helping others, which I find enormously rewarding. Peter was awarded the CBE in the New Year's Honours List, 2000 and was knighted four years later, making him Sir Peter and me his lady!

The reader may be interested to know that the house we live in today is a big cottage, chocolate box picture perfect and the house of my dreams. I was right: cottages suit me very well. Peter and I have danced the Viennese waltz in a gilded and mirrored ballroom filled with pink carnations in a palace in Vienna and it was every bit as magical as I thought it would be. We have had a wonderful holiday in Mauritius, where I thought I was in Heaven; the people are delightful and an example to the world that different races and religions can live together in harmony. We visit Churchill College often; it makes us feel young again, and we enjoy dining there. I still love being up at night when most people are asleep; it's a good time for thinking and writing.

Gill married Henry in November 1971 and initially continued to work in theatres in various hospitals. She trained for her District Nursing Certificate and became a district nursing sister in London. Henry went on to complete his training as a doctor and then they moved to the South West where he became a GP. They had three girls. Gill chose not to return to nursing and retrained as a school librarian, a job she loved. Gill and Henry are enjoying retirement and seeing more of their five grandchildren.

Liz worked briefly as a staff nurse before settling down and raising her family of five children. A year after the birth of their twins, Liz and Paul separated and later divorced. After several years working in Podiatry, Liz returned to nursing and enjoyed many years working in the community as a staff nurse until her retirement. After twenty years together, Liz and Mike finally married in 2010 and Liz has five lively grandchildren to enjoy. Paul died in 2010.

Angie worked as a staff nurse on Paget (women's medical) and then left to do her midwifery training. She returned to Addenbrooke's to staff on Musgrave (women's surgical) and moved with the ward to the New Site where it was called D8. The old names were abandoned. She married Eric, 'the boyfriend from home', in 1974. They had two children and have five grandchildren. Angie returned to work at her local hospital, first on Gynaecology, and then on a special care baby unit where she stayed until her retirement.

Rita worked for a while on Victoria (women's surgical), but made her escape to go travelling. She worked picking grapefruit on a kibbutz in Israel, but then got a wonderful job dancing in films. Returning to England, she intended to train as a teacher in dance and drama, but met John and followed him to Germany instead. They were married in 1975. They moved to Wales and had two girls. Rita ran a smallholding for ten years, but then returned to dental nursing, which she had done for a year before starting her student nursing. They have four grandchildren.

Annie moved to London with Nigel, who continued his medical training, specialised in genitourinary surgery and worked as a consultant surgeon until his retirement. Meanwhile Annie became a qualified midwife. They were married in 1973, but Annie continued to work, first as a ward sister on ENT and women's surgical. Next she gained a year's experience in occupational health. They had two boys, and later Annie returned to work part-time as a bank nurse and then in an outpatient department until her retirement.

Dawn, as we predicted, was the most ambitious nurse of all of us. She continued working at Addenbrooke's Hospital and became Ward Sister on a sixty-six bedded mixed surgical ward and then a nurse consultant in Breast Disease. She achieved a BSc and MSc in Advanced Clinical Practice and served on various national working parties like the Prime Minister's Commission for the Future of Nursing and Midwifery and the Cancer Strategy Working Group. Also she became the breast nurse advisor to the charity Breakthrough. She was awarded the MBE for Services to Breast Cancer Care and Nursing in the New Year's Honours List, 2008.

The Eightsome, and many others from our set, continued in various fields of nursing and they attend our reunions in Cambridge. Initially these were every ten years, but are now every five. The first one was held in Brown's Restaurant, which we jokingly pointed out is situated where the venereal disease clinic used to be.

In 1972 the remaining wards at the Old Site moved to Hills Road to become part of the new hospital. No longer were medical and surgical patients and babies all nursed together on one Children's Ward. I was privileged to be Staff Nurse at a special time.

The façade of the Old Site was listed and is now the front of the Judge Institute building. On a tour inside we were delighted to discover an old Nightingale ward fireplace has been retained amidst the stunning, colourful, modern architecture.

The Addenbrooke's Hospital complex at Hills Road is huge and continues to grow. It is the size of a small town, complete with shops, cafés and banks. Recently a new road was opened linking it directly to the M11. The Trauma Unit has been featured on television and is a far cry from the Accident Service we knew, but it stands as a brilliant illustration that Addenbrooke's is still a hospital at the forefront of medical care and we are all very proud to have been a part of its history.

I hope you have enjoyed my book. If you would like more information, or to comment, or leave a review, please visit my website: www.eileengershon.com